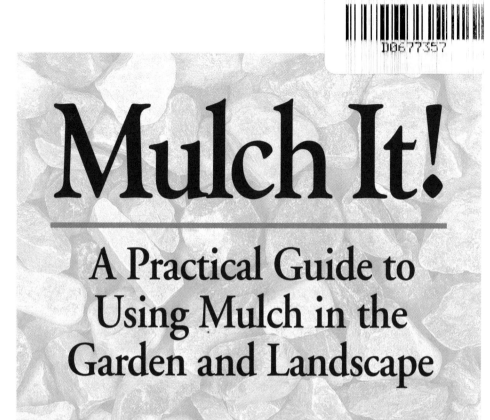

Mulch It!

A Practical Guide to Using Mulch in the Garden and Landscape

STU CAMPBELL

Storey Books, Inc.
Schoolhouse Road
Pownal, Vermont 05261

The mission of Storey Communications is to serve our customers
by publishing practical information that encourages personal independence
in harmony with the environment.

Revised and updated by Charlotte Kidd
Edited by Gwen W. Steege and Larry Shea
Cover design by Leslie Constantino
Text design by Susan Bernier
Text production by Deborah Daly and Jennifer Jepson Smith
Cover photos by Giles Prett
Cover illustrations by Artville
Illustrations by Alison Kolesar
Indexed by Peggy Holloway

Printed in the United States by Versa Press
10 9 8 7 6 5 4 3 2 1

Library of Congress Cataloging-in-Publication Data

Campbell, Stu.
    Mulch it!: a practical guide to using mulch in the garden and landscape/Stu Campbell.
        p. cm.
    ISBN 1-58017-316-0 (alk. paper)
    1. Mulching. I. Title.
    S661.5 .C353 2001
    635'.04-dc21   00-063484

contents

PART I

THE WHY AND WHATS OF MULCHING

MORE REASONS THAN EVER TO MULCH

R ich looking, neat as a pin, weed free, and glowing with health — does that sound like the yard or garden of your dreams? It can easily be a reality if you use mulch. Once thought of primarily for vegetable gardens, mulch has come a long way. It's now recognized as an essential ingredient for more beautiful and easier-to-maintain flower beds and landscape plantings of all kinds. And in addition to beautifying your property, mulch has many important environmental benefits as well, one of the most important of which is water conservation.

Our water supply is finite and often unevenly distributed. Some gardeners may experience water shortages and brush fires, while others are building levees and raised beds. Although mulches may not do much to control excess moisture, they are essential in the battle against water loss. They are so important, in fact, that California enacted a bill requiring the use of mulches: the Xeriscape Act of 1989.

Xeriscaping is a garden design principle whose aim is to reduce the amount of water used on landscapes. While the idea of conserving water in the garden has been around for some time, the xeriscape concept was refined by the Denver Water Department in 1981, after a particularly dry summer. The department developed what have become the seven basic principles of xeriscaping: proper planning and design, limited use of turf areas, use of efficient irrigation systems, soil improvements, *mulching*, use of plants that demand less water, and appropriate maintenance (such as weeding and fertilizing). This concept quickly spread to Florida, Texas, Arizona, and California, where droughts are a fact of life. The National Xeriscaping Council, Inc., has been established in Austin, Texas, to coordinate and promote the xeriscaping movement. After all that, who would need to be convinced to use mulches?

It seems, though, that mulching does require more justification for some. For one thing, *mulch* doesn't even *sound* very nice, which may be one strike against it to begin with. In its earliest Middle English sense, the word *mulsh* was an adjective that meant, according to Mr. Webster, "soft or yielding." That's not so bad. But by the time our language had evolved into what is now called Early Modern English, centuries later, the "s" in *mulsh* had become a "c," the adjective had become a noun, the word itself had come to mean "rotten hay," and something pleasant was lost in the evolution.

Now this is to suggest neither that rotten hay is *necessarily* undesirable nor that rotten hay is the only kind of mulch there is. There are many, many kinds of materials that can be used for mulching, as we shall see. The mulch materials you choose for your vegetable garden can be practical, but not necessarily beautiful. On the other hand, you'll find dozens of choices for mulching around your landscape plantings and flower beds where the mulch itself can be an important feature of the overall design. Whatever the choice, to the knowledgeable gardener, mulch can be the most beautiful stuff in the world.

A neatly mulched garden can bring many rewards.

A LIVELY DEBATE

You'll soon learn that mulching needs justification among serious and experienced gardeners, too. It is awfully hard to imagine at first glance that a subject like mulching could be very controversial. I mean, either you like to mulch your garden or you don't, right? Not so. Highly regarded gardening authorities like Ruth Stout, known to many gardeners as the "complete mulcher," and Leonard Wickenden, a prominent biochemist and thoroughly experienced organic gardener, sparked a mulching debate that has carried on in gardening literature for years. Some people don't know with whom to side, so they don't bother to mulch at all. We'll have a look at each of their points of view a little later on.

Some vegetable gardeners object to mulching for purely aesthetic reasons. They prefer the traditional look of arrow-straight rows and bare, immaculately cultivated earth. There still are plenty of these "model" gardens around, and that sort of thing is fine if you have lots of time and patience, plenty of water, and maybe a few slave laborers who can help you maintain this kind of elegance. Most of us do not. Let's face it: except for the very affluent, the days of the full-time hired gardener are gone forever. Besides, mulch does not *have* to be unattractive, as we shall also see.

Because my garden is in a northern section of the United States, I know that what works well for me may not work well for you in your garden. You also should remember that there is no one "right" way and no one "wrong" way to mulch. There are good ways, and there are not-so-good ways. This book offers suggestions about *some* ways to mulch your gardens to make them happier, healthier, and more rewarding. I will also try to make you aware of certain dangers and pitfalls, but I will never say, "This is *the* way." That is for you to decide.

2

HERE'S WHY:
The Benefits of Mulching

Mulching has many benefits, not the least of which, as far as I'm concerned, is that you can walk around in your garden on rainy days and not have 3 inches of sticky mud on the soles of your shoes when you come back inside. I choose to ignore the experts' warnings to stay completely out of the garden on wet days. I am careful not to touch anything, mindful that I might be transmitting some harmful bacteria or virus to the plants. And I try to stay in the middle of my mulched path so I don't compact the soil near my plants. But it seems to be a compulsive ritual with me to go into my garden at least once a day. I need to squat down next to a row and gently (sometimes not so gently) try to coax young seedlings into growing faster, bigger, or greener. Not a scientific argument for mulching, I know, but certainly an emotional one.

For mulching's technical benefits, I turned to Dr. Donald Rakow, Professor of Landscape Horticulture at Cornell University. According to Dr. Rakow, mulch's three major benefits are reducing water loss from the soil, suppressing the growth of weeds, and protecting the soil from temperature extremes.

MULCH RETAINS MOISTURE

Mulch's ability to conserve soil moisture has long been documented. While authorities and test results differ, it is clear that mulch reduces moisture evaporation from soil by anywhere from 10 to 50 percent. Mulch's water-conserving value can't be overemphasized, especially during times of water restrictions, shortages, and drought conditions.

Mulch keeps soil from drying out partly because it prevents dew and water, drawn up from the subsoil, from escaping. Contrary to what many believe, dew is not only water condensation from the atmosphere; it is also moisture condensation from air pockets in the soil. As far as plant growth is concerned, most dew is completely wasted unless there is something on the surface to catch it and prevent it from evaporating.

MULCH'S BENEFITS: THE BIG THREE

► Reduces water loss

► Suppresses weeds

► Insulates against hot and cold

Some impervious mulches, like black plastic or old boards, may catch more dew because they don't allow air to pass through. The downside is that they also don't let water or air in. That's something to keep in mind when selecting a type of mulch. More on that later.

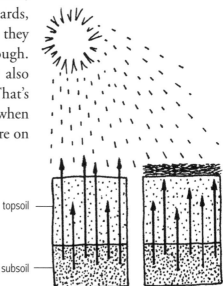

Mulch keeps soil from drying out by inhibiting evaporation of dew and moisture that is drawn up from the subsoil by capillary action.

topsoil —

subsoil —

MULCH SUPPRESSES WEEDS

Mulching can practically eliminate the need for weeding and cultivating. Imagine how much extra time that will leave you for picking strawberries, lying in the hammock, or visiting other gardeners!

There are a few catches, however. First, the mulch itself must be weed free. Many a gardener's best mulching intentions have gone astray with one application of weed-strewn hay or manure. Rather than controlling weeds, they ended up introducing a whole new pesky weed crop.

Second, mulch must be deep enough to prevent existing weed seeds from taking root. Weed seedlings need light to grow. Weeds sprouting under a dark blanket of mulch wither away without light. If mulch is applied too thinly, weeds may still poke through. So when you mulch, be as persistent as a weed and cover all open areas.

Finally, mulches won't smother all weeds. Some particularly tough weeds have the fortitude to push through just about any barrier. In a well-mulched bed, though, these intruders should be easy to spot and even more easily plucked.

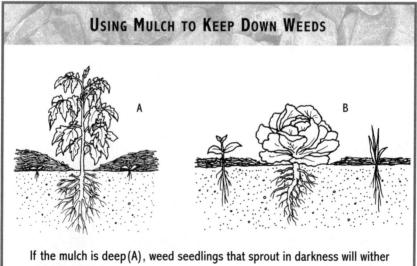

USING MULCH TO KEEP DOWN WEEDS

A   B

If the mulch is deep (A), weed seedlings that sprout in darkness will wither away. If a mulch is too thin (B), some weeds will poke through. Even then, they are easy to spot and easy to pull.

MULCH INSULATES FROM HEAT AND COLD

Mulch's ability to regulate soil temperature is probably one of the benefits most often overlooked, especially by first-time gardeners. Many of us are so concerned with aboveground temperatures that we don't spend much time pondering what's happening underground.

Simply stated, mulch is insulation. It keeps the soil around your plants' roots cooler during hot days and warmer during cool nights.

In winter, mulch works to prevent soil from alternately freezing and thawing, which leads to soil heaving and root damage. Now this doesn't mean the soil won't freeze; it just won't happen overnight. Rapid freeze-thaw changes not only threaten aboveground growth, they also may send tender plant roots into shock. That's why it's best to apply winter mulches in the fall, after a good frost when the plants are dormant. Come spring's warm weather, be sure to remove the mulch when plants start sprouting new growth.

On the other hand, mulches are useful for controlling soil temperatures in summer. These are frequently referred to as "growing" or "cultural" mulches. Applied in the spring after the soil starts to warm up, they stay in place for the majority of the growing season.

Extremely high soil temperatures can inhibit root growth and damage some shallow-rooted plants. During the long, hot days of summer, a mulch can reduce soil temperature by as much as 10°F.

Some plants, though, thrive in heat. Besides organic mulches, there are special synthetic mulches for them. Tomatoes, eggplants, and peppers appreciate high temperatures. Black or red plastic around tomatoes has been shown to increase fruit yields.

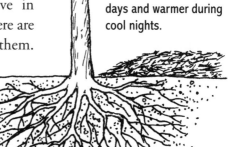

Mulch is insulation. It keeps soil around plant roots cooler during hot days and warmer during cool nights.

You can remove some or all of an organic mulch at the end of the season. Most types are usually incorporated right into the soil — which leads us to some of the other benefits of mulching.

MULCH CONTROLS
EROSION AND IMPROVES SOIL

Mulching prevents soil compaction and crusting by absorbing the impact of falling raindrops. Water penetrates through loose, granulated soil but runs off hard, compacted earth. Mulch controls wind and water erosion by slowing water runoff. Mulch helps to hold soil in place — a benefit for the ornamental perennial bed as well as the steep slope. This is why you see newly grassed banks along highways covered with mulch. It keeps the dust down, too.

Organic mulch can be a soil conditioner. Some soil that might normally break up into chunks when tilled or cultivated will crumble into fine granules after even just a few weeks under a bio-degrading mulch.

Many organic mulches, like shredded leaves and bark chips, add organic material to soil as they decompose. This leads to all sorts of great things. Enhanced soil structure, for example, improves aeration, water percolation, and nutrient movement throughout the soil.

Mulching encourages earthworms, which further aerate the soil and release nutrients in the form of "castings." Earthworms should be considered prominent citizens in any garden! They are particularly important in perennial beds and rarely plowed or tilled garden plots. Mulching keeps your soil friable and hospitable to earthworms, who'll gladly do much of the underground work for you.

MORE ADVANTAGES OF USING MULCH

► Improves soil

► Helps keep plants healthy

► Organic mulch adds soil nutrients

► Benefits the environment

► Looks good

Mulch stimulates increased microbial activity in the soil. Certain bacteria are every bit as important as worms. Microbes break down organic matter rapidly, making plant nutrients available to roots sooner. This means, as Ruth Stout suggests, that your garden is operating very much like a compost heap.

Mulch Helps Grow Healthy Plants

Mulched plants are less diseased and more uniform than those without mulch. One reason is that mulching prevents fruits, flowers, and other plant parts from being splashed by mud and water. Besides causing unsightly spots and rot, splashing can carry soilborne diseases. Mulch protects ripening vegetables, like tomatoes, melons, pumpkins, and squash, from direct contact with the soil. That means fewer "bad" spots, rotten places, and mold.

Although the jury is still out on whether mulches help control harmful soil nematodes or fungi, there is some evidence that a few light-reflective types, such as aluminum foil and polyethylene film, may reduce aphid and leaf miner populations and some diseases that they spread.

Basically, mulching helps reduce plant stress. Healthy, strong plants have the energy and resources to better protect themselves against insects and other pests.

Organic Mulch Increases Soil Nutrients

Organic mulch can increase available potassium by allowing it to attach to the decaying mulch instead of to the soil particles. When fixed to the soil, a good deal of potassium isn't accessible to a plant. Depending on their age, type, and duration of exposure, mulches can also contribute nitrogen, phosphorus, and several trace elements to the soil chemistry.

Mulches aren't dependable as a primary plant food, though. Dr. Rakow suggests supplementing mulched areas with other fertilizer because mulch alone may not be enough. Herbaceous plantings may actually show signs of chlorosis without an additional feeding or two of fertilizer.

MULCH IS ENVIRONMENTALLY BENEFICIAL

Using mulches for weed control helps reduce our dependence on chemical herbicides. The fewer chemicals we use, the lower the risk of groundwater contamination, general exposure to toxins, and accidental poisonings.

Mulching is an excellent way to reduce and recycle yard waste. Even if you live on a quarter acre of land and have a small garden, you generate tremendous amounts of waste in and around your home. Rather than burning leaves or carting cut grass off to a landfill, use them! Dead (not diseased or insect-infested) plants, leaves, grass clippings, old newspapers — just about anything is fair game for the mulch pile. Even larger woody materials can be converted into mulch with a portable chopper or shredder. But be sure not to add poison ivy, sumac, or oak to your mulch. And don't reuse diseased or insect-infested materials; they'll only spread the problem. Thoughtful recycling helps your plants and the environment at the same time.

MULCH IS ATTRACTIVE

While they don't have the most scientific of reasons, many folks mulch just because they like the way it looks. Ask your friends why they mulch. I'll bet they won't say "to free up my soil potassium." They will probably say mulching makes their gardens look a little better or neater. Or maybe they just like the color or texture a certain mulch lends to their landscape. Mulching an ornamental bed with shredded bark or hardwood gives it a professional touch.

3

GIVE THE DEVILS THEIR DUE:
Some Drawbacks to Mulching

Before you rush out and start mulching the neighborhood, I should introduce you to a few of the controversies associated with mulching. Mulching is not a new phenomenon, and neither is arguing about it. For example, it was on a chilly spring morning more than 40 years ago now that a lady in Connecticut named Ruth Stout, who had both a very green thumb and a way with words, wandered into her garden and felt the ever-so-faint stirrings beneath her feet that only people who are attuned to such things can feel. Little did she know, I would guess, that right then and there, as the seeds of three famous gardening books *(How to Have a Green Thumb without an Aching Back, Gardening without Work,* and *The No-Work Garden Book)* began to germinate in her fertile mind, that she was about to single-handedly revive and popularize the ancient art of mulching.

THE STOUT SYSTEM

The Stout complete-mulching system is very simple. This is how she described it in *The No-Work Garden Book:*

> *. . . I was, as usual, trying to be patient until someone could do some plowing for me, when finally one day, I used my head. No, not for plowing — for reasoning. My asparagus was doing beautifully and I said to myself: that ground hasn't been plowed for over ten years; what has asparagus got that peas haven't? To heck with plowing! I'm going to plant. . . .*
>
> *. . . After putting hay all over the garden I soon found that the only jobs left were planting, thinning, and picking. Whenever I wanted to put in some seeds, I raked the mulch back and planted, and later, when the seeds had sprouted, I pulled the mulch close around the little plants, thus keeping them moist and outwitting the weeds. . . .*
> *. . . My plot has become so rich now that I can plant very closely, and I don't even use manure or chemical fertilizer. The garden is one-eighth its original size and so luxuriant that in the fall we call it the jungle. . . .*

Stout was really a sheet composter who used no machinery. "Make your garden your compost pile," she writes in *How to Have a Green Thumb without an Aching Back*. "My way is simply to keep a thick mulch of any vegetable matter that rots on both my garden and flower garden all year round." A compost heap is too much trouble, she says. Just spread mulch where you eventually would have spread the compost anyway. In time it will rot and become rich dirt. In fact, she would go so far as to say in *The No-Work Garden Book* that if you were to cover sod with a heavy layer of mulch in the fall, you could make plantings there — without plowing, tilling, or spading of any kind — the following spring. Stout also writes:

> *F*or the past twenty-six years I have used no fertilizer of any kind on any part of my garden except rotting mulch and cottonseed meal. I broadcast the latter in the winter at the rate of five pounds to every one hundred square feet of my plot. I'm not really convinced that my soil needs the meal, but I have been told it does for nitrogen.
>
> However, if gardeners weren't driving in here quite often to inspect my system, I think I would skip the cotton-seed meal for a season and see if it made any difference. But as long as I am exhibiting the excellent results which I get from my method, with so little work, I can't afford to have a failure.

This experiment made years ago verified Ruth Stout's theories about mulch on top of sod. Thick layers of hay were laid on a plot of grass in the fall. In the spring plantings could be — and were — made there. The soil was moist and soft and needed only to be scuffed with a hoe and rake. No plowing or tilling had to be done.

Ruth Stout represents a charming antithesis to the kind of quasi-scientific approach to vegetable gardening that spewed reams of complicated, pamphletized data and contradictory advice from various headquarters of state university extension services throughout the country during the late 1940s and 1950s.

Stout often leaves herself wide open to the criticism that she oversimplifies. Perhaps she does, but her reassuring advice to the neophyte gardener who is faced with the apparent complexities of mulching would be: Don't worry about it! What about hay seeds in the mulch, you ask? If the mulch is thick enough, she would answer, the weeds won't come through. When do you start mulching, then, you might counter? "Anytime!"

THE ATTACK

Along came Leonard Wickenden, the gardener's organic gardener, who didn't buy Ruth Stout's act. In his encyclopedic *Gardening with Nature*, in which he relies heavily on his own scientific background, his immense horticultural experiences, and his own intuitive organic gardening sense, he jumps on mulching with both feet. He writes, in only slightly veiled reference to Mrs. Stout:

> *Here we have a practice that has gained greatly in popularity in recent years. . . . The soil between rows of crops is covered with a layer of straw, coarse hay, sawdust, or trash of some kind. It is claimed for this practice that it retains moisture by checking evaporation, keeps down weeds, prevents undue baking of the soil and encourages the growth of earthworms. There is much truth in these claims. Weeds are by no means entirely eliminated, but those that make their way through the mulch are easily*

uprooted. Evaporation is checked and the soil kept cool, which means that earthworms will remain nearer the surface, although it does not necessarily follow that their numbers will increase.

But there is another side of the picture. If soil is covered by, let us say, coarse hay, much of any rain that falls on it will be held by the hay. Since this rain will be spread in a thin film over the fibers, it will evaporate readily and the soil below will never get the benefits of it. In other words, whatever may be gained by retaining moisture already in the ground may be counterbalanced by what is lost in the subsequent rainfall.

It is also a question whether the protection of the soil is entirely beneficial. Certainly in the spring every gardener longs for the warm sunshine to raise the temperature of his soil and so speed up the growth of his seedlings. At what point do we decide the soil is getting too much warmth?

Finally, there is the danger that natural forces and conditions will start converting the mulch into sheet compost. . . . This is likely to rob the soil of nitrogen. It is particularly likely to occur in a wet season when both the mulch and soil in contact with it are continuously damp and thus favorable to the growth of microorganisms.

. . . The advantages and disadvantages of mulching depend on the climate of the location and the weather of the season. If a mulch could be applied at the beginning of a dry spell and removed at the beginning of a wet one, its value could probably be great. Since that is impracticable there is no clear indication of its value and the matter becomes one of personal judgement.

THE REBUTTAL

Ruth Stout's response is characteristically unscientific: her rebuttal in *Gardening without Work:*

> **H**e [Leonard Wickenden] admits that he had never mulched his garden, yet he goes bravely ahead and explains what's 'wrong' with the idea. He says, 'Weeds are by no means entirely eliminated,' which is misleading, for he certainly gives the impression that he is talking about all, or at least most weeds. The fact is that if you mulch deeply enough all weeds are eliminated except a few perennials. . . .
>
> Next Mr. Wickenden states that if a garden is mulched, light rains will do it little or no good because the moisture will be spread out in a thin film over the hay and will evaporate. Since he doesn't mulch, he must be speaking from theory only, which reminds me that according to all the known laws of physics, bumblebees can't fly, yet they keep right on at it.
>
> . . . Mr. Wickenden also declares that the ground needs the direct sun in the spring to warm it up, but I have found this to be true only in those sections where the earliest crops are to be planted. And since you have to pull the mulch aside anyway in order to plant, it isn't extra work to push it back ahead of time and let the sun reach the soil. Of course you have to be blessed with a mind which can figure that out. . . .

Sorting It Out

If you are not entirely convinced by Ruth Stout's rebuttal, let me put in my two cents worth. I'll try not to be so emotional.

Moisture. First, to answer Mr. Wickenden's questions: Won't mulch prevent rain from getting to the soil? Yes, but not in the way he suggests. Coarse hay, which he chooses as an example, is one mulch that water penetrates easily. Water does seem to spread in a "thin film" on the fibers, but beads of water will collect rapidly and dribble through the mulch to the soil below. In fact, in this way the soil is moistened for a while after a light rain shower has stopped.

Matted leaves, dry-crusted peat moss, or very finely chopped hay spread too thickly can inhibit or even prevent any water penetration. Chopped leaves seem to allow more water through. Peat moss is less absorbent and less likely to crust if it is mixed with something else, like pine needles or even surface soil. The problem presented by any impermeable artificial mulch is solved easily: Poke some holes in it to let water through to the soil!

On the other hand, is it good for mulch and soil to be damp continuously? Yes. You might find it somewhat moldy under there, but all indications are that this does no damage to the soil or to the plants. Damping off is *not* a threat to healthy, well-established plants. If damping off is a problem in your area, do not mulch too closely around very young plants.

Light. Shouldn't the soil get sunshine? I referred this question to microbiologist Dr. Doug Taff. He thought for a moment and said, "I don't see why. Look at a tropical rain forest. Roots and soil there never see sunlight."

Certainly, to germinate a seed needs sunshine for warmth, but the sunshine needn't be full strength. (I don't advocate planting most small seeds under heavy mulch anyway.) It is possible that sunlight on the soil could prevent some diseases from spreading, but at the same time it would reduce beneficial microbial activity. Don't forget: The action is in the green leaves of plants, where photosynthesis, which requires sunlight, takes place — not in the roots (although important things happen there, too). Naturally, all green leaves should be kept above any mulch.

Heat. At what point do we decide that the soil is getting too much heat? Soil that is overheated can cause root damage. It is conceivable that soil might get too hot under black plastic in particularly warm climates — although proponents of black plastic mulch insist that the heat from the dark surface is given off to the atmosphere above the plastic, not to the ground beneath. It is my feeling that most worries about the soil overheating under organic mulch are unwarranted. Organic matter is good insulation that discourages extremes in soil temperature.

PROBLEMS AND SOLUTIONS

The vast majority of my own experiences directly contradict the claims of Mr. Wickenden. Don't get me wrong. There are some things to consider when deciding whether to mulch. But I believe with every problem comes a solution. Let's look at these considerations one by one.

Mulch Controls but Doesn't Eliminate Weeds

It's true that mulches can't smother every weed. Robust perennial weeds have been known to push up through straw, wood chips, and black plastic. Heck, they've been known to emerge out of a concrete sidewalk.

Solution. Mulching makes it easier to pull out the darned things. Remember, mulching is not meant to eliminate all your gardening chores. It simply makes them easier. And I'm sure if I really wanted to prove a point, I could choke out just about any weed if I buried it under enough mulch.

Certain Mulches Create Nitrogen Deficiencies

Any fresh, light-colored, unweathered organic mulch will steal nitrogen from plants during the earliest stages of decomposition. Wood-based products, such as sawdust or wood chips, are routinely condemned for this, but hay, straw, and leaves also tie up nitrogen. Eventually, though, these will add nutrients to the soil as they decay.

Solution. To deal with the temporary nitrogen shortage, supplement your gardens with additional nitrogen. Ruth Stout, you'll recall, fertilized with cottonseed meal, which is rich in nitrogen. Or try alfalfa meal (if you can afford it) or one of the chemical nitrogen sources like calcium nitrate or urea.

Some Mulches Inhibit Water Penetration

The knock against black plastic has always been its inability to let rainwater through to the soil and, ultimately, to the roots. The same can be said for some organic types of mulch, like leaves, if they get matted down.

Solution. If you decide to use plastics, be sure to moisten the ground thoroughly first. Place the mulch down and make slits or holes in the vicinity of your plants to allow for watering. That will expose those areas to weed growth, so you may have to pull a couple of stragglers now and then. Still, I'd rather pull a handful of "volunteers" than weed out a whole bed.

As for matted leaves, chopping them beforehand is the best prevention. For other compacted organic mulches, turn or loosen them occasionally to allow water to reach the soil and plant roots.

Some Mulches Block Airflow

Another knock on black plastic. I guess that's why the new permeable landscape fabrics have become so popular. Even organic mulches applied too deeply or repeatedly can restrict air movement into the soil. Roots need air to breathe. Many beneficial microorganisms that break down nutrients absorbed by roots need air to live.

Solution. It's a good practice to get in there and stir things up occasionally. Loosen the crust with a hoe or rake. If you plan on supplementing your mulch because it has lost some of its color and appeal, be careful not to overdo it. Sometimes we add another 4 inches of mulch when we need only 1 inch to freshen the appearance. Remember, overmulching can kill your plants.

Mulch Is a Breeding Ground for Insects, Slugs, and Snails

I have to admit that when I look into the mulch in my own garden I feel like a giant parting the trees of some miniature rain forest. The decaying, rich-smelling organic mulches are alive with all sorts of creepy-crawling insect things, most of which I can't identify. Most of these guys aren't doing any harm. Their job is to break down the organic stuff so the plants can absorb the nutrients. I just leave them to their creeping and crawling and put the mulch back where it was.

You will find an increase in the slug and snail populations when you use mulches, particularly in years with a wet spring. These wet, slimy creatures love the dark, damp areas under a mulch, whether it's organic or black plastic. These fellows can have a field day feasting on your plants and definitely warrant a little attention.

Solution. One suggestion is to pull back the mulch and sprinkle the slugs with salt. Or you can try one of the chemical slug controls on the market. Drowning slugs in yogurt cups half-filled with diluted beer is another option.

I have found that a light dusting of wood ashes or diatomaceous earth on the ground at the base of my plants works well. The slugs and snails don't like to crawl over these materials because they are abrasive to their underbellies. Both will need to be reapplied regularly because they deteriorate with rainfall.

Mulch Is Unpleasant and Difficult to Handle

Here I must agree with Mr. Wickenden. Mulching *is* a matter of personal judgment. Selecting and applying the wrong mulch for your situation can be a big headache.

On the other hand, applying an appropriate mulch early in the growing season frees up a lot of time and hassle later. And a winter mulch application may keep roses and some woodies from perishing in the freeze/thaw cycle. This is why I recommend becoming familiar with a wide range of possibilities. If your mulching repertoire is wide enough to allow you to choose the right place for the right mulch at the right time, you can enhance your garden's attractiveness and productivity with a minimum of effort, time, and money.

Solution. If you don't have time or just aren't up to the work, there are garden care professionals who will gladly deliver and apply mulch to your ornamental beds. For vegetable and small gardens, how about hiring a teenager or local agricultural student to give you a hand? The cost will be minimal compared to the labor saved weeding and watering in the summer heat!

Mulch Attracts Rodents

Mice and other rodents drawn to the warmth and protection of a thick mulch may take up residence there during the cold winter months. As food supplies dwindle, they may elect to gnaw on your favorite fruit tree.

Solution. To prevent this, never apply an organic mulch all the way up against the base of your trees or shrubs. Leave 6 to 12 inches of space between the mulch and the tree or shrub. If the mice are going to feed on your tree, they'll have to come out in the cold to do it! To be really sure they don't damage your plant, you may want to put a wire shield around the base. Quarter-inch hardware cloth works quite well.

Dry Mulch Is a Fire Hazard

Some mulches, like sawdust, are particularly susceptible to spontaneous combustion. A spark dropped into a peat moss mulch can cause a fire to smolder unnoticed for hours and can be difficult to extinguish. Very dry hay and wheat straw can also catch fire easily.

Solution. It seems obvious to me that you need to be careful around these mulches. Don't smoke near them, and during extraordinarily dry periods water them occasionally.

4

A FEW
DEFINITIONS

I find that many good gardeners — probably because they like to garden more than they like to study the technicalities of gardening — use gardening terms rather loosely. Ask 10 gardeners to define a word like *mulch* or *compost* and you will get the proverbial 10 different answers. Interestingly enough, in the particular case of these two words (compost and mulch), the varying descriptions are not only confusing, they frequently overlap and are sometimes reversed.

Here seems a good place to explain some terms already mentioned. These are not meant to be strict, inflexible definitions. In fact, you may disagree with them totally. They are offered simply as working definitions to describe what I mean when I use a particular word. Let's start with *compost*.

Compost is organic matter undergoing or resulting from a heat-fermentation process. This heating, generated by intense bacterial activity, may develop temperatures as high as 150 or 160°F near the center of the compost pile. Heat is the factor distinguishing compost from mulch. In other words, if the material has not heated, it is not compost.

Humus is dark, rich, well-decomposed organic material. The end result of all composting (and mulching, eventually) is humus. When garden topsoil contains a generous amount of humus, the garden is probably fertile, productive, and full of plump worms. Rotting organic matter cannot be considered humus until you no longer can identify the original compost material. Humus is the ultimate and highly coveted by-product of thoroughly decomposed mulch as well as compost.

Mulch can be any material applied to the soil surface to retain moisture, insulate and stabilize the soil, protect plants, and control weeds. A properly functioning mulch has two basic properties. Good mulch should be 1) light and open enough to permit the passage of water and air and 2) dense enough to inhibit or even choke weed growth.

Mulches can be divided into two fundamental categories:

1. Organic mulches are like unfinished, unheated compost. Any biodegradable material (anything that will rot) can be used as organic mulch. Organic mulches are preferred for the noncommercial home gardener. Vegetable matter is better than something like old cedar shingles, planks, or magazines and newspapers — although these do make effective mulches if you don't mind seeing them in your garden.

IS IT MULCH OR IS IT COMPOST?

Mulch

- ▶ Organic or artificial material
- ▶ Unheated, 2- to 4-inch blanketlike layers
- ▶ Use on top of soil to inhibit weeds, conserve moisture, control erosion, and stabilize soil temperature

Compost

- ▶ Heat-fermented organic material
- ▶ Large piles hot with microbial activity
- ▶ Use mixed with topdressing or as soil amendment to provide food for microbes, worms, and plants

---

The most common organic mulches are shredded or chipped bark, leaves and leaf mold, hay, straw, grass clippings, and by-products like cocoa hulls, ground corncobs, and spent hops from breweries.

2. Inorganic mulches, sometimes called inert or artificial mulches, don't begin as plant material. They can be substances that never rot, such as colored plastics, or they can be mineral products like crushed stone and gravel chips. Another example of inorganic mulch is geotextile landscape fabric, spun-bonded or woven from polypropylene or polyester, cut for and used as mulch.

Universities and the agricultural industry are continually researching the pros and cons of colored plastics on small fruit and vegetable crop production, so keep your eyes peeled for the most current information. In the meantime, I've included the latest on plastics, geotextiles, and more in chapter 5.

Here are a few other terms associated with mulching that are sometimes bandied about:

Summer mulches, or growing mulches, are applied in the spring *after* the soil starts to warm. Throughout the summer, they insulate the soil, inhibit weed growth, retain moisture, and control erosion. Both organic and artificial mulches fall into this category.

Winter mulches are used around woody plants and perennials to insulate against freeze-thaw damage to plants' crowns and roots. Winter mulch is applied in late fall *after* the soil has cooled, preferably following a hard frost. The idea is to keep the soil temperature from jumping up and down and heaving plants out of the ground. Ordinarily, winter mulches are organic, but geotextiles may provide adequate winter protection.

Living mulches are low-growing, shallow-rooted, ever-spreading ground cover plants like vinca, myrtle, thyme, sweet woodruff, English ivy, and pachysandra. These mulch plants are attractive and commonly used in border flower beds, ornamental plantings, and rock gardens, but they can be effective in the food garden as well.

Permanent mulches are usually made up of nondisintegrating (not necessarily nonbiodegradable) materials. Permanent mulches like crushed stone, gravel, marble chips, and calcine clay particles are useful, particularly in perennial beds, around trees and shrubs, and on soil not likely to be tilled or cultivated.

Green manures (green-growing mulch) are basically cover crops like ryegrass, alfalfa, and buckwheat that meet the definition of mulch. They afford fine winter and erosion protection with the added

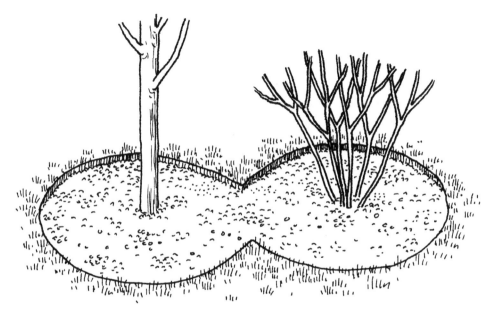

A permanent mulch of stone works well around trees and shrubs.

advantage of attracting beneficial insects during the growing season. They can be tilled under as sheet compost or harvested and applied as mulch in another part of the garden. Cover crops are used mostly in vegetable gardens or small fruit plantings.

Sheet composting is when a layer of organic matter (alfalfa stalks or leaves, for example) is laid on the top of the growing surface and then worked into the earth by plow, rototiller, or spade. Once covered or partially covered with dirt, the organic matter decomposes very rapidly but without heat.

Homemade mulches usually consist of plant-based materials gleaned from household refuse, especially from the garden. They include dry coffee grounds, tea leaves, chopped paper, stringy pea pods, and wilted Swiss chard leaves. Vegetable leavings, if not tossed on the compost heap, are fine to throw directly on the garden. (No meat, bones, fat, or dairy products, though; these will attract critters.) If this somehow offends you or might upset a neighbor, discreetly tuck the vegetable discards under the mulch already there. Who's to know? Neighborhood dogs, incidentally, are not attracted to coffee grounds, for example, if they are buried under so much mulch that no scent can escape. Homemade mulches are historically popular with vegetable gardeners. With the ease of chipper/shredders, many home gardeners are creating their own landscape mulches from pruned branches and fallen leaves.

Feeding mulches will rapidly add plant food to your soil. Rotted leaves, manures, and compost (compost can also be used as mulch) are the most obvious kinds of feeding mulches.

Seed-free mulches are just what the name implies: organic mulch that has not yet or never will go to seed. This can include hay that has not blossomed or is sterile. With a seed-free mulch, there is no danger of donating potential weeds to your garden.

I hope this chapter has cleared up a few things so that the rest of the book will make sense. Please refer back to it whenever necessary.

5

TYPES OF MULCH

Broadly speaking, mulches are organic and biodegradable or are made of other substances such as stone or plastic. Depending on the material, mulch can be decorative, functional, or both. Biodegradable organic mulches conserve soil moisture and, in varying degrees, add nutrients to the soil. Stones and most inorganic mulches don't improve a soil's health or water retention. Organic and inorganic mulches both largely provide weed and erosion control.

Following are descriptions of many common and uncommon mulches, beginning with biodegradable organic mulches in the categories of bark and wood products, plant products, and specialty and regional mulches. After addressing these I'll discuss some soil amendments that can be used as mulches, paper mulches, and a variety of other, mostly inorganic mulches you might want to try.

BARK AND WOOD PRODUCTS

In response to the Clean Air Act of 1972, the lumber industry looked for ways to recycle (rather than burn) its by-products. As a result, bark and wood chips found alternative value as landscape and general garden mulch. The National Bark and Soil Producers Association (NBSPA) sets industry guidelines for soil as well as mulch from wood products. By 2001, the NBSPA expects to have a voluntary industry certification program to ensure the quality of commercially sold mulches and soils. Chapter 7 contains more information about landscape mulch.

▷ BARK AND NUGGETS

Uses. Decorative and functional

What they are. Bark is probably the most common and versatile of the landscape mulches. You can usually find bark mulches in a variety of shapes, sizes, colors, and textures. Bark, the tree's cambium layer, is composed of lignin, which acts as a tree's armor. Lignin decomposes more slowly and is less appealing to insects than cellulose, the tree's heartwood. Barks such as cypress and hemlock are naturally insect resistant. The best ornamental mulch contains at least 85 percent shredded bark.

Bark mulch can be from conifers such as pine, or hardwoods such as oak. Recommended varieties of bark and wood mulch are listed on page 30. Bark mulch comes in several sizes (from ¼ inch to 3 inches in diameter) and forms (shredded, various-sized chips, nuggets, and mininuggets). Bark mulch is sold in 3-cubic-foot bags or in bulk by the cubic yard.

How to use them. Prepare the garden bed by adding soil amendments. Install plants, and water thoroughly and deeply. Then apply mulch like a blanket over the plant's existing or potential roots. Cover the entire bed evenly with a mulch layer 2 to 4 inches thick for weed control and moisture conservation. Because mulch against a plant stem or tree trunk will invite rot and insects, move mulch material several inches away from direct contact with the plant. Keep mulch at least 6 inches away from the base of a woody shrub or a tree trunk.

Pros. Readily available in many forms. Attractive. Because it decomposes slowly, bark mulch is less hospitable to artillery fungus.

> ## A CHIP OFF THE OLD BLOCK
>
> I have a friend who used to sell firewood in the Northeast, and he spent big money on a machine that could debark his trees before cutting them up. When I asked him why he went to all the trouble, he said he made more money from the bark chips than he did from the firewood.

❯ CORK

Uses. Decorative and functional

What it is. Ground cork, as you might expect, is extremely light and easy to handle. It is *so* light, in fact, that you might also expect that the first breeze would blow it across the countryside and that even a raindrop would dislodge it from place. Surprisingly enough, it stays in place very well once it has been soaked.

Dry or wet, ground cork is completely odorless. Its disintegration is so incredibly slow that it seems like an inert material. It is hardly possible to measure its effect on the soil's nitrogen content.

How to use it. Like bark, cork can be raked, saved, and used from one season to the next.

Pros. Cork has always been known for its insulating qualities, so it comes as no surprise that ground cork is excellent in this respect.

Cons. It is not easy to find cork unless you live near a large cork producer, and it might be expensive.

❯ EVERGREEN BOUGHS

Use. Functional

What they are. Boughs of conifers are probably more attractive as Christmas decorations than as mulch. But they are valuable winter protection, especially around newly planted perennials, roses, and shrubs; on outdoor containers; and over a bed of spring-flowering bulbs. The Georgia Extension Service recommends them for erosion prevention, too.

How to use them. After the ground is frozen for the winter, lay boughs loosely over garden beds, container plantings, perennials, and bulbs and at the bases of shrubs and small trees. Remove boughs in early spring, when sprouts start poking from the ground. Replace them with nutritious leaf, bark, or root mulch.

► Sawdust

Use. Functional

What it is. Sawdust refers to the tiny, dustlike wood particles left after wood is sawed.

How to use it. Sawdust is frequently recommended as a mulch under blueberries, rhododendrons, and other acid-loving plants. Unweathered pine sawdust decomposes very slowly, so just give it some time to weather and turn gray before you use it. Hardwood

---

WHICH WOOD IS THAT ANYWAY?
BARK/WOOD MULCH VARIETIES

Cedar: Bark and/or wood from trees of the genus *Thuja*

Cypress: An insect-resistant fibrous mulch used mainly in Florida, Georgia, Louisiana, and Ohio. Its matting quality is useful for erosion control.

Douglas fir bark: Insect-resistant bark mostly available in the Northwest

Eucalyptus: Ground, shredded hardwood from the bark and trunk of the plantation-grown *Eucalyptus viminalis*

Hardwood: Bark and/or wood from deciduous hardwood trees

Hemlock bark: Insect-resistant bark from the genus *Tsuga*

Oak bark: Insect-resistant bark from genus *Quercus*

Pine bark: Conifers of genus *Pinus*

Redwood bark: Real and imitation types are available. Real redwood bark, which is insect-, disease-, and rot-resistant, comes from the Coast Redwood *(Sequoia sempervirens)* on the West Coast. Also, Eco-Safe Mulch, an imitation redwood bark made of various wood chips dyed red, is widely available.

Stump and root: Products derived from processed tree stumps and/or roots

Western: Bark and/or wood from conifers of western North America

---

sawdust, by the way, rots much more rapidly than pine or spruce or cedar sawdust, especially if it is weathered. You can also combine sawdust with other mulching materials to improve water penetration and reduce compaction problems. Simply turn over the mulch now and then to get air into it and break up the big chunks. No more than an inch or two of sawdust mulch is needed around most plants.

Cons. Because it decomposes so slowly and seems to discourage earthworms, sawdust is not your best choice for a vegetable mulch. Water penetration through sawdust is only fair. In fact, some gardeners complain that sawdust mulch actually draws moisture out of the soil. Others believe are that sawdust packs down quickly and appears to be toxic, causing plants to turn yellow and suffer. Sawdust is not toxic. Fresh sawdust does, however, have a very high carbon content. You soil scientists out there know that a high carbon content ties up the nitrogen in a soil. Soil microorganisms become overly concerned with breaking down the sawdust, and you end up with nitrogen-deficient plants.

Add extra nitrogen fertilizer, such as calcium nitrate or ammonium nitrate, to mulched areas to counter the nitrogen deficiency. Be careful not to overdo it: Too much nitrogen can be harmful to plants, too. Nitrogen is highly soluble in water, and excess may leach away and end up in the groundwater.

➤ SHREDDED WOOD WASTE

Use. Functional

What it is. Shredded wood waste includes untreated, unpainted woody debris from construction and land-clearing operations that's processed into coarse "chips" sold as Hog Fuel (presumably named after the grinding machine known as a *hog*). Shredded wood waste in King County, Washington, is used for mud control and as mulch for large-scale commercial landscaping projects.

How to use it. The "fine" grade material is preferred for horticultural mulch and soil amendment. The 2-inch particles allow water into the soil. Apply as directed. To offset nitrogen loss in decomposition, add nitrogen to planting areas.

▷ Wood Chips

Uses. Decorative and functional

What they are. Wood chips from a brush chipper generally make excellent mulch. Commercially prepared wood chips are available by the bag and truckload. At the New York Botanical Gardens in the Bronx, wood chip mulch is stolen from beneath plants faster than the gardeners can put it there. That's how popular wood chips are.

Colorized wood chips from recycled wood are popular in red, yellow, black, and natural. Some types (Eco-Safe Mulch, for example) are chipped, shredded, then dyed red with an environmentally safe coloring to maintain color longer than most natural mulches. Don't confuse this with redwood mulch from trees native to the West Coast. Goldentone Mulch is also made from recycled wood, then dyed yellow.

How to use them. Wood chips are often used on garden paths because they don't tend to become compacted by foot traffic. For your garden, apply a 2- to 4-inch layer like a blanket over the soil around your annuals, perennials, and vegetable plants. For trees and shrubs, first remove grass and weeds from under the branch canopy. Spread an even layer of wood chips, 2 to 4 inches thick, under the branch spread. Keep chips at least 6 inches away from the plant base.

Pros. Wood chips are economical and commercially available in different hardwood and softwood varieties by bag and bulk. Utility companies in some areas will sometimes offer free excess wood chips from pruning operations.

Cons. Chips don't stay in place as well as barks and may blow or float away. As with sawdust and other wood products, wood chips have a high carbon-to-nitrogen ratio, so they temporarily tie up nitrogen during decomposition. Add some nitrogen before planting in soil previously covered with wood chips.

Some folks tend to overmulch with wood chips. Because wood chips lose their color and decorative appearance much more quickly than bark chips, they add a new layer every year. But most don't remove any of the old layer first and end up with 5 or 6 inches of mulch where they wanted only 2 or 3 inches. This overmulching can choke out shallow-rooted plants and promote canker growth on susceptible trees and shrubs. To avoid this, rejuvenate your chips every two or three years and add no more than you actually need to give them a fresh look.

▷ WOOD SHAVINGS

Use. Functional

What they are. Wood shavings are the thinly curled stuff you sweep off the floor next to a cabinetmaker's bench. They might also be the fluffy shredded wooden packing material sometimes called *excelsior.*

How to use them. Mix hardwood shavings with cottonseed meal, alfalfa meal, or a high-nitrogen commercial fertilizer.

Cons. Softwood shavings from pine, cedar, and spruce are notoriously voracious nitrogen thieves: The thinnest shavings are the worst offenders. I recommend chips over shavings if you like the idea of using a wood-based mulch.

OTHER PLANT PRODUCTS

Mulches in this category range from ubiquitous — and essentially free — grass clippings and leaves to more unusual mulches, such as salt hay.

▷ CORNCOBS AND CORNSTALKS

Use. Functional

What they are. Midwestern gardeners have known for a long time that ground corncobs and stalks make a fine mulching material.

How to use them. Ground corncobs may generate heat after a while. So keep them away from the stems of tender young things. A 3- to 4-inch layer usually is enough. Discard stalks infested with borers, disease, or worms.

Pros. Ground cobs are an excellent weed inhibitor and do a good job retaining soil moisture.

Cons. The texture of corncob mulch doesn't allow rainwater into the soil. Cornstalk mulch won't win any prizes for attractiveness, but it might make a great conversation piece when the garden club comes to visit.

▷ GRASS CLIPPINGS

Use. Functional

What they are. Almost anyone with a yard has grass clippings, so they are probably the most frequently mentioned garden mulch.

How to use them. Dried clippings are useful as a thinly spread mulch as your first vegetable seedlings come up. Some gardeners like to mix grass clippings with peat moss to slow down a very rapid rate of decomposition.

Pros. Besides providing good nutrients, the fine grass will not choke the tiny plants the way a thicker, coarser mulch might. Overall, grass clippings are good, cheap mulch. They are already chopped if you use a rotary lawn mower.

Cons. Spread too thickly, clipped grass will make a hot, slimy mess and smell bad. Don't recycle clippings from a lawn with a sizable population of noxious weeds, like dandelion, crabgrass, or plantain, or grass that's gone to seed — unless you want to spread the weeds. And don't reuse clippings treated with herbicide within the last three weeks; it's just not worth the risk.

▷ GREEN LIVING GROUND COVERS

Uses. Decorative and functional

What they are. These low-growing plants include thyme, myrtle, oregano, perennial vinca, and ivy for sun; pachysandra, sweet woodruff, and ginger for shade. Violets and Johnny-jump-ups thrive in all sorts of conditions. Perennial geraniums such as 'Biokovo' and 'Lancastriense' form handsome, expanding, semievergreen clumps with beautiful spring-into-summer blossoms and coppery fall foliage.

How to use them. Creeping perennials are easy care and self-sustaining in places where you don't walk a lot. Just plant in good soil, water, fertilize occasionally, and watch them take off. A few weeds may sprout until the ground cover becomes firmly entrenched. Then these creeping perennials will grow so thick that nothing else has a chance.

Pros. Excellent appearance. Persistent spreader. Easy to transplant.

Cons. Expensive.

PACK IN THE PACHYSANDRA

Pachysandra is expensive, spreads slowly but persistently in shady, moist conditions, and is easy to transplant. To begin or expand a patch, find a friend who has plenty and wants to share the bounty. Removing six or eight plants is like taking a bucket of water out of a well — no one will ever notice they are gone. Place the stems and roots where you want the new growth. Cover the roots with soil, then water and keep somewhat moist until they show small new green leaves.

▷ GREEN MANURE (A.K.A. COVER CROPS)

Use. Functional

What it is. Buckwheat, annual ryegrass, and winter rye are examples of conventional cover crops farmers know well. More and more vegetable gardeners are discovering the benefits of green manure such as alfalfa, winter peas, soybeans, and clover. Green manure can be annual or perennial depending on your plant choices. A number of garden seed catalogs offer a good variety to choose from.

How to use it. Vegetable gardeners often sow a green manure after harvesting their crops to fill in bare spots. Small fruit growers who plan in advance may use cover crops. The cover crop remains in the garden over the winter and is tilled under the following spring.

Pros. Besides keeping weeds at bay, green manure decomposes to add nutrients to the soil. Legumes such as alfalfa and clover also fix nitrogen. The U.S. Department of Agriculture describes one study using winter annual legume hairy vetch (*Vicia villosa* 'Roth') both as a cover crop and as a mulch in sustainable tomato production. As a cover, vetch fixes nitrogen, recycles nutrients, reduces soil erosion and compaction, and adds organic matter to the soil. When converted to a mulch, the vetch reduces weeds, increases organic material, reduces water loss, and acts as a slow-release fertilizer.

Many traditional cover crops also encourage beneficial insects, a plus for any Integrated Pest Management effort.

➤ HAY

Use. Functional

What it is. Hay probably has been used longer than any other mulching material. Chopped hay is less unsightly than loose hay. Seedless hay is desirable for mulching raspberries, grapes, and young fruit trees. Make friends with a local farmer, who may be glad to get rid of hay that has spoiled and is unfit to feed to livestock. Have you noticed how much cut hay (some of it is weeds) there is along the sides of public roads in late summer? Rake it up! It's free for the taking.

First-cut hay is normally hay that has been allowed to go to seed. Many gardeners are reluctant to use it as mulch because it introduces a horde of weed and grass seeds into the garden. Ruth Stout argues that if the mulch is kept thick enough — as much as 8 to 10 inches — very few weeds will surface, regardless of the number of seeds in the mulch. Usually you don't have to add more hay. Lift what is already there, fluff it, and put it back down on top of the weeds.

Second- or third-cut hay often is harvested before it goes to seed. So you might feel a little better about using this on your garden.

How to use it. See Ruth Stout's System (page 12). Partially rotted hay makes better mulch than fresh hay. Leave some fresh bales outside through the winter; by spring they will be weathered and damp.

Pros. All hay decomposes fairly rapidly and boosts the soil's nitrogen content.

Cons. Fresh hay will steal nitrogen for a short time when it begins to rot.

➤ LEAVES

Use. Functional

What they are. It seems almost criminal to burn leaves or send them to the dump — they are nature's favorite mulching material. Leaves contain many essential trace mineral elements that the long, penetrating tree roots have retrieved from the deep subsoil. Besides the basic nutrients that all plants need — nitrogen, phosphorus, and potassium — leaves also have small amounts of minerals such as boron, cobalt, and magnesium.

How to use them. Chop those leaves up to speed decomposition and prevent soggy mats of leaves. Spread 2 to 4 inches of chopped, decomposing leaves on any garden. Or use 2 to 3 inches of decaying leaves, then top with 1 or 2 inches of an attractive shredded bark mulch.

If raking leaves is a dreaded chore, try mowing them with a mower that has a bagging attachment. That chops them so you can carry them away in one easy step. Some people put leaves in a big trash barrel, then whip them into shape with a string trimmer. Another strategy is mixing leaves with straw, ground corncobs, pine needles, or other light material to improve the mulch's consistency.

Pros. Look up and down; leaves are all over the place. And they make a splendid mulch in any state of decomposition. Oak, beech, and sycamore leaves don't mat too badly but are more satisfactory if chopped. Chopped leaves allow water and air to penetrate easily, which lessens the danger of crown rot in some plants.

Cons. Chopped leaves take a bit of extra work. Maple, birch, and elm leaves tend to mat and become soggy. Whole, matted leaves don't let water reach the soil where your plants can use it.

⟩ LEAF MOLD

Use. Functional

What it is. Leaves vs. leaf mold? Leaf mold has disintegrated to the point where the leaves are no longer distinguishable; you have crumbly humus and the leaf's skeletal system. Rich leaf mold is so nutritious that it's especially good for plants that are difficult to cultivate, such as grapes, berries, and fruit trees.

THE LIFE CYCLE OF A LEAF

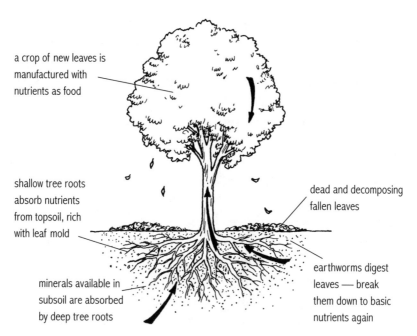

a crop of new leaves is manufactured with nutrients as food

shallow tree roots absorb nutrients from topsoil, rich with leaf mold

minerals available in subsoil are absorbed by deep tree roots

dead and decomposing fallen leaves

earthworms digest leaves — break them down to basic nutrients again

Leaves, in any state of decomposition, make excellent mulch. They contain many essential trace mineral elements that the long, penetrating tree roots have retrieved from the subsoil. In addition to the basic nutrients that all plants need — nitrogen, phosphorus, and potassium — leaves also have such minerals as boron, cobalt, and magnesium.

How to use it. Apply like any other organic mulch. Leaf mold mixed into the soil before seed planting can produce a spectacular effect on many plants' growth.

Pros. Leaf mold is chock full of nutrients and microbes ready to nurture any plants you decide to treat with the best of nature's gifts.

▷ PINE NEEDLES

Use. Functional

What they are. Pine needles, also called pine straw, are widely available for the raking. They are light, clean, weed free, and easy to handle. In the southern United States, gardeners can buy baled pine straw. Loblolly, slash, and long leaf are the most common pine needles.

How to use them. Rake into a mulch layer 4 to 5 inches deep; it will settle to about 2 inches. White pine trees have soft, flexible needles that make fine mulch. Needles from the red pine are coarser and may not rot for several years; they are good for mulching larger plants. Cedar trees drop fine but wider "leaves" that make a great mulch for windy places. If you have ever tried sweeping them off a roof or walkway, you know about their affinity for staying put.

Pine needles are especially good for mulching small fruits such as strawberries and blueberries. It is traditional to use them around acid-loving plants, but they do not lower the soil pH too much for you to use them on other plants as well.

Pros. Pine needles absorb little or no moisture, so water trickles easily through them. They can be used more than once because they decompose so slowly.

Cons. There is little worm activity under pine needle mulch.

▷ STRAW

Use. Functional

What it is. Ideally, straw should be seed free and chopped. Straw from timothy, oats, barley, wheat, and rye is widely available and relatively cheap. It can be used as a summer mulch around vegetables or as winter protection for trees, shrubs, and strawberries. It's frequently used by homeowners trying to start a new lawn.

How to use it. A layer of chopped straw needs to be only about 1½ inches thick. Loose straw can be as much as 6 to 8 inches thick but does not give a very tidy appearance. In either case, unless the straw is well weathered, add some high-nitrogen fertilizer to the soil first.

Cons. Straw can be a fire hazard. Also, straw is a common bedding material around the farm, so it's not unusual to find little creatures, like mice and voles, setting up camp in a deep straw mulch. If you do use straw around your favorite plants, don't lay it right up against their base.

SPECIALTY AND REGIONAL ORGANIC MULCHES

Depending on where you live, these mulches may not be easy to find. You might think it was worth the effort, though, when you have the only garden beds on your block that are covered with fragrant cocoa hulls or attractive crushed oyster shells.

▶ BUCKWHEAT HULLS

Uses. Decorative and functional

What they are. Buckwheat hulls, popular as pillow and bedding filler, are expensive, in short supply, and used selectively as mulch when available. The New Alchemy Institute in Falmouth, Massachusetts, touts buckwheat hull mulch, a by-product of its usual grain crop, as both aesthetically appealing and an effective weed suppressant. If you can get buckwheat hulls, give them a try.

How to use them. They usually are applied in a layer 1 to 3 inches thick. A 50-pound bag will cover 65 square feet at a 1-inch depth.

Pros. I have heard several gardeners call this "the ideal mulch." It handles easily, decomposes slowly, and does just about everything a mulch is supposed to do. It is inconspicuous and can be raked up in the fall and saved for another season.

Cons. A buckwheat hull mulch does not retain soil moisture as well as some other mulches do. It also can be blown around in a heavy wind and splashed about in a real downpour. Because the hulls are dark, they absorb heat and can burn the leaves of succulent young plants that grow close to the ground. They are expensive.

▷ COCOA HULLS

Uses. Decorative and functional

What they are. Cocoa hulls are the outer shells winnowed from roasted cocoa beans in preparation for making chocolate. They're available in areas that are near a chocolate-processing factory, like Hershey, Pennsylvania. After you open the bag, the hulls give off a chocolate smell in your garden!

How to use them. Cocoa hulls come by the bag. They shovel easily, so it takes little effort to apply a 2- to 3-inch layer of hulls around your plants. Donald Rakow, a landscape horticulturist at Cornell University, cautions homeowners that the high potassium content of cocoa hulls may be toxic to some ornamentals.

Pros. Because cocoa hulls are dark in color, they absorb heat and warm the earth beneath them. They decompose slowly, adding lots of nitrogen, phosphorus, and potassium to the soil as they rot. They are very light and are an attractively rich brown when first spread.

Cons. Cocoa shells or hulls retain moisture for long periods and get slimy to walk on after about six months in the open. They may pack, too, and during periods of high humidity may develop molds on their surface. These molds are harmless and can be put out of sight simply by turning the mulch. One measure for preventing such visible mold is to improve the mulch's texture by mixing in two parts shells to one part sawdust or pine needles.

Unless you happen to live near a chocolate-processing factory, you may have to forget using cocoa hulls. They are expensive, so they may be best reserved for only the most visible flower beds and rose gardens.

▷ COTTONSEED HULLS

Uses. Decorative and functional

What they are. Cottonseed hulls are plentiful and cheap, particularly if you live near a cotton gin in one of the southern states. They are a by-product of cotton and cottonseed processing.

How to use them. These hulls can be used most effectively around plants such as beans, which are suited to wide-row planting. (We plant bean and pea seeds four to six abreast in 10- to 12-inch-wide rows.) Apply in a 1- to 2-inch layer. Or you can wait until the plants have grown 3 or 4 inches high, then sift the mulch down through the leaves, keeping weeds down in hard-to-reach places.

Pros. Cottonseed hulls have a fertilizer value similar to, though not as rich as, that of cottonseed meal.

Cons. Because they are so light, the hulls blow around in the wind.

▷ CRANBERRY VINES

Use. Functional

What they are. Cranberry vines are sold commercially on Cape Cod and in Wisconsin, New Jersey, and other places where cranberries are grown.

How to use them. Vines can be used whole (they are a little unwieldy this way) or chopped. They are good looking either way. For winter protection, you might want to hold cranberry vines in place with evergreen boughs.

Pros. They are wiry and light and never pack down. They decompose very slowly, so they can be used over and over again. Pea vines have similar characteristics.

▷ EUCALYPTUS

Uses. Decorative and functional

What it is. Eucalyptus mulch is the ground, shredded hardwood from the *Eucalyptus viminalis* in Florida and California. It's plantation grown. The bark and trunk are processed for mulch; the top branches are used for cogeneration fuel.

How to use it. Eucalyptus mulch is shredded and fibrous. Its color and texture make it excellent for topping off container plantings, as well as for giving a professional touch to ornamental beds. Apply in a 2- to 4-inch layer, like a blanket, as with other organic mulches.

Pros. Eucalyptus mulch is nicely textured and an attractive brown. Although not as aromatic as the leaves, it smells fresh. It retains moisture and won't float or blow away. Because it's resinous, it is said to repel insects such as ants.

▷ HOPS

Use. Functional

What they are. Spent hops, just a waste product as far as a brewery is concerned, make an inexpensive mulch where available.

How to use it. Apply it 4 inches thick, rake it up later, and save.

Pros. Hops decay very slowly, so they need to be renewed only every three or four years. They are resistant to fire because the plant material tends to stay damp; they make an ideal mulch for conserving soil moisture.

Cons. At first, you might find that hops have an objectionable odor. Spent hops mulch also can generate an overdose of heat, so keep it a little farther away from very small plants. There is yet another odd drawback to spent hops — one to consider if you live in an urban area. Hops are very hard to keep in place because pigeons — believe it or not — find some food material in them that they enjoy. The birds will pick the plants over continually and spread hops all over yard and lawn. This was such a problem in a botanical garden in Boston that the gardeners were forced to quit using hops as a mulch.

▷ LICORICE ROOT

Uses. Decorative and functional

What it is. Licorice root mulch is available on the East Coast as a by-product of a Camden, New Jersey, industry. Fibrous and dark, the root is what's left after a company processes plants for extract for pharmaceuticals, cosmetics, tobacco, and sweeteners. The licorice plants arrive in bales from Afghanistan, Russia, China, Saudi Arabia, and Syria.

How to use it. Open bags and fork or shovel licorice root onto the garden bed between the plants. Layer like a blanket, 2 to 4 inches high. As with all mulches, keep away from stems, trunks, and branches. It usually lasts for one gardening season.

Pros. It is attractive and relatively easy to apply. Although the price can seem high, do your comparison shopping. At peak season, there are often rebates and sales for large-quantity purchases.

Cons. Bagged licorice root has a strong odor that quickly disperses after the mulch is spread.

⟩ MELALEUCA TREE

Use. Functional

What it is. An invasive tree imported from Australia, the melaleuca (tea tree) is damaging the Florida Everglades. It is crowding out native species, and its roots are draining water from the glades, so it's become an environmental problem. To control the invasion, people in southern states are encouraged to use this tree as mulch.

How to use. Organic mulches containing melaleuca are available commercially. Apply in a 2- to 4-inch, even layer.

⟩ OYSTER SHELLS

Uses. Decorative and functional

What they are. Oyster shells are crushed shells from those delicious mollusks. Oyster and clamshell mulch is quite popular in shore areas.

How to use them. If recycling whole shells, wash them first. Apply and crush as you wish. They're also available commercially in bags. Just open the bag and shovel them onto the soil around the root area in a 2- to 3-inch layer.

Pros. Oyster shells are "basic," or "alkaline." This means they have a high pH and operate like lime to neutralize acid soils. This mulch therefore works well on soils with a low pH.

THE OYSTER ANSWER

Ruth Bixler had trouble keeping anything growing in the shale soil of her Pennsylvania home. She says, "One Saturday I stopped at the feed store to get some food for our rabbit, and right in front of me I saw the answer — bags of ground oyster shells. I bought bag after bag and started shaking it over my soil. I really put it on thick and it was beautiful for the summer; not even a heavy shower disturbed it. . . . The roses were never more beautiful and bloomed until the first snow. . . . My Mimosa trees got through the severe winter without a single loss."

⟩ PEANUT HULLS

Uses. Decorative and functional

What they are. Peanut hulls are available throughout much of the southern United States. Alone, they make an attractive, coarse-looking mulch.

How to use them. Sometimes they are mixed with sawdust or pine needles. Peanut hulls have many fine qualities as a mulch. Use them if they are available where you live.

Pros. They weather quickly, decompose rapidly, and add good, rich, humus to the soil. They contain considerable amounts of nitrogen, phosphorus, and potassium. According to some studies, they make a very good mulch for tomato plants.

Cons. They might be attractive to rodents if not completely free of peanuts.

⟩ RICE HULLS

Use. Functional

What they are. Rice hull mulch isn't unusual in regions that use rice as a food staple. In hot, dry weather, rice hull mulch develops a crust that discourages chickens from bothering your garden.

How to use them. Forming rice hulls into a kind of bowl around each plant makes watering easier, because the crust they form causes water to run off to the plants' roots.

⟩ SALT HAY

Use. Functional

What it is. Salt hay consists mostly of grasses harvested from salt marshes in coastal areas that, for plant conservation reasons, should be left alone. In New England, there's a salt hay and hay substitute called Mainely Mulch made from sterile, dehydrated, and heat-processed hay and straw.

How to use it. As salt hay carries no weed seeds, gardeners prefer it to hay for vegetable gardens. It makes an exceptionally good winter mulch. A bale of salt hay will provide a 3- to 6-inch covering for an area of about 1,200 square feet.

Pros. Salt hay or salt straw is light, clean, pest free, and long lasting. It can be used a second or third time. Water penetrates it easily so it seldom gets matted or soggy.

Cons. Salt hay is almost impossible to get; don't kill yourself trying to find it. There are plenty of other mulches that are cheaper and no threat to the environment.

▷ SUGARCANE

Use. Functional

What it is. Sugarcane residue, often called *bagasse*, consists of cane stalks that have been pressed, heated, and ground. Sometimes it is packaged and sold under the name Servall.

How to use it. Its pH is somewhere between 4.5 and 5.2, so it might be a good idea to add a little lime to your soil if your plans include extensive use of bagasse mulch.

Pros. Cost is moderate.

Cons. Sugarcane never seems to weather or darken but retains its very light color, which some people find objectionable. Like peat moss, it is highly absorbent and will hold about three-and-one-half times its weight in water. Other than that, it makes a pretty satisfactory mulch. Bagasse rots quickly because of the sugar content, so it needs frequent replenishment.

▷ WALNUT SHELLS

Uses. Decorative and functional

What they are. Ground or whole walnut shells last a long time. Pecan and almond shells are very much the same. All are cinnamon brown in color and have a pleasing appearance.

How to use them. An inch or two of walnut shells is plenty. Use the shells for several years.

Pros. They don't wash away and are fire- and rot resistant. They absorb very little moisture, so water percolation into the soil is good. Walnut and pecan shell mulches also might furnish some good minerals during their super slow rotting process.

SOIL AMENDMENTS AS MULCH

One benefit of mulch, you'll remember, is improving the soil. As it happens, some materials often used to amend soil can be mulches as well. You'll have to decide in each case, though, whether the material is best worked into the soil or used as a surface mulch.

COFFEE GROUNDS

Use. Functional

What they are. Coffee grounds are a good homemade mulch, even though it will take a while to accumulate enough to do you any good (unless you drink an awful lot of coffee). Used grounds have a very fine consistency and will cake once they are exposed to the elements.

How to use them. Use them lightly — never more than an inch deep — or else air may not be able to reach the plant roots. I'd say coffee grounds are most appropriately spread in containers and the vegetable garden or else sent to the compost pile.

Cons. They aren't too flattering to ornamental plantings and might not be the best possible choice for placing around the family's favorite tree.

COMPOST

Use. Functional

What it is. Compost is a combination of green and brown organic materials, such as leaves, grass, and other vegetable matter. Partially decomposed compost, of course, is a fantastic feeding mulch. In the garden it disintegrates quickly to become humus, adding many nutrients in the process.

Pros. Inexpensive. Improves soil and invites earthworms.

Cons. I regard the relative cost of a compost mulch as high. Good compost always is in great demand, and supplies almost always seem to be limited. If your compost-mulch is made up primarily of leaves, it may become matted if you ignore it for too long without turning it. If that happens, water won't be able to pass through it.

MANURE

Use. Functional

What it is. Manure is animal excrement, usually from herbivorous farm animals, such as horses, cows, and chickens. Most of us think of manure more as a fertilizer than as a mulch, but it supplies all kinds of plant food and can fulfill many requirements of a good mulch. Most animal manures are mixed with straw, sawdust, or some other absorptive material used as bedding. Stables, friends with horses, and agricultural schools are good sources of free manure.

How to use it. The best manure is well rotted. Don't forget: If you use good, well-rotted manure as mulch, it will encourage weed growth just as much as it encourages any plant growth. You may have to pull a few weeds or top with a different mulch.

Pros. Improves soil.

Cons. Fresh, unaged manure can burn plants and will smell awful. Be a little careful with the dried, packaged varieties, too. They have been known to contain harmful salts.

MUCK

Use. Functional

What it is. Muck is black organic matter retrieved from swampy areas. Its characteristics are similar to those of sludge, another highly fertile material that is the product of sewage treatment plants. Muck sometimes is packaged in polyethylene bags and sold commercially.

Cons. Once it dries it becomes a fine dust that can blow around or be washed away by rain. Muck also disintegrates fast and needs to be replenished often. Both of these negative qualities can be improved if you mix muck with something else to make it denser.

PEAT MOSS

Uses. Decorative and functional

What it is. Mention the word "mulch" to someone and he will possibly reply automatically, "Oh yes, you mean peat moss." Peat moss and mulching are synonymous in many people's minds.

Peat moss is partially decayed, humus-rich plant matter from waterlogged soils, such as those in bogs. There's some controversy about whether peat moss is being removed in larger amounts than its bogs can sustain.

Pros. Peat moss aerates the soil.

Cons. Peat moss dries out quickly, crusts over, and isn't easy to rewet. It is extremely slow to decompose. It is slightly acidic but does not sour your soil unless used continuously and in great quantities. It has practically zero value as an organic fertilizer. Find something better — and cheaper — to use as mulch.

▷ POULTRY LITTER

Use. Functional

What it is. Poultry litter might be composed of straw, sawdust, shavings, and crushed corncobs, plus the manure itself, but it is primarily the manure in this concoction that supplies nitrogen to the soil. The fact that it *is* a mixture is important. Straight manure might damage plants by giving them an overdose of nitrogen.

Pros. Poultry litter still is widely available at low cost from many poultry farms.

Cons. Bad odor.

▷ PROCESSED SLUDGE

Use. Functional

What it is. Many municipalities recycle dry materials (biosolids) in community wastewater into a usable by-product: processed sludge. Land application of biosolids has been a common commercial farming practice. The U.S. Department of Environmental Protection and state environmental agencies regulate its use. Federal and state governments also set standards for treating the processed sludge material now available free or at low cost to the homeowner, gardener, and landscaper.

How to use it. Before using processed sludge as mulch, check with your local environmental protection agency or agricultural extension for regulations and recommended uses in your area. As the product quality (including toxicity and plant nutrient components) varies, it's best to be current with your information. In some cases, processed sludge mixed with wood products and other dilutants may be okay for overall landscaping or a seldom-worked bed of woody plants but not for vegetable gardening.

Pros. Processed sludge is cheap and available. Treated for pathogens and composted with bulking materials, such as wood chips and sawdust, biosolids are a rich source of soil nutrients.

Cons. Though designated as acceptable for mulch, processed sludge alone can release sufficient ammonia to damage plants. For public use, some municipalities mix it with yard wastes and wood chips.

That mix can contain unwanted litter, weed seeds, and who knows what else. It often has a distinctive odor that's difficult to remove from gloves, clothing, and shoes. It can be mucky and may stain clothing.

❯ SEAWEED (KELP)

Use. Functional

What it is. Kelp is seaweed. There doesn't seem to be any way that seaweed will improve the look of your garden unless it is finely chopped.

How to use it. If the kelp gathered on the beach is loaded with salt, you might do well to rinse it off once or twice with your garden hose. But don't worry about getting it entirely salt free. What salt is left probably will benefit rather than harm your soil.

Pros. Seaweed decays into potash, among other things. It also provides sodium, boron, iodine, and other trace elements. It is an excellent winter mulch and a great material for sheet composting. In most coastal areas it is free. In meal and liquid concentrate form, kelp is an exceptional fertilizer full of macro- and micronutrients; processed kelp is pricey but well worth the cost.

Paper Mulches

Paper is cellulose, which decays easily. Paper as mulch can come in many forms: from the common newspaper recycled for the garden to commercial mulch paper to treated felt.

Paper produced specifically to be used as mulch was first developed for pineapple plantations in Hawaii. Treated to make it waterproof, it is particularly valuable as a weed controller. I'm sorry to say that special farm equipment is needed to lay it neatly and efficiently over large areas, but the backyard gardener can manage it with a little patience.

▷ BIODEGRADABLE BLACK PAPER

Use. Functional

What it is. This nifty product comes in different widths and has a line of neat round holes cut down the center of the roll.

How to use it. Place plants in those neat holes. It seems to work in much the same way as black polyethylene and is certainly no more difficult to hold in place than plastic.

Pros. It stays intact throughout the growing season.

Cons. It may not decompose on its own as readily as the manufacturer indicates. Once over lightly with a rototiller pulverizes it. It is not advertised as having any particular fertilizer value, and I have not seen any analysis of exactly what it contains.

▷ FELT PAPER

Use. Functional

What it is. My experiments with roofing paper or tar paper were discouraging because the material was so difficult to hold in place without tearing.

How to use it. Builders' "felt" paper, which is not so brittle, can be laid with some success next to early tomato transplants.

Pros. It will absorb heat and warm the soil around the roots.

Cons. I wouldn't run out and buy roofing paper exclusively to use in the garden; it's expensive and not very practical. If you have some lying around the basement and want to use it up, do so with care. Some chemicals used in manufacturing are toxic to some plants.

NEWSPAPER

Use. Functional

What it is. The home gardener can use shredded paper as mulch. Newspaper, for example, is an organic material and some inks provide trace elements essential to healthy plant life. Mulching with waste paper offers a great opportunity to recycle those stacks of newspapers gathering dust in your basement.

How to use it. Try shredding newspaper with your lawn mower. It may not be particularly attractive, but it looks better than newspaper laid in folded sheets between rows of plants. It is also more permeable to water. Paper mulch can be covered with a little soil or wood chips to hide it and keep it in place. I know someone who uses newspaper to cover her entire garden, covers that with hay, then pokes holes through it with a ski pole to plant seeds. When everything is picked in the fall, she simply tills the whole works under.

PAPER PULP

Use. Functional

What it is. Convert waste paper, sawdust, and other trash into a mobile, flowing slurry by combining it with water and grinding it up. Years ago someone developed a machine called the Garbamat, which was like a gigantic garbage disposal, for just this purpose. The invention never was widely distributed, but the stuff it produced was found to be a very fertile mulch and was used as a side-dressing.

How to use it. Paper pulp is used quite often in the hydroseeding process; it's the green stuff you see road crews and large landscapers spraying all over bare soil. It's a mixture of grass seed, paper pulp, nutrients, and water. It is particularly popular on sloping areas and in housing developments. The only reason it's green is so the landscaper can see where it has been applied. I also have seen some hot pink hydroseeding mixes used for wildflowers.

Pros. The paper disintegrates, adding humus to the soil.

LAYING COMMERCIAL MULCH PAPER

A

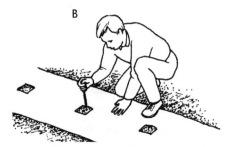

B

Lay the paper by hand and cut holes (A).

Prepare the soil beneath the holes with a small tool (B).

C

Add fertilizer mixed with water and transplant. Be sure that all the edges of the paper are well covered with soil (C).

OTHER MULCHES

The following mulches — which include geotextiles, plastic mulch, and stone — are mostly inorganic, so they're not going to add a lot to your soil. Some of them might be just the right choice, though, for conserving water, warming the soil, and serious weed prevention.

▶ ALUMINUM FOIL

Use. Functional

What it is. Aluminum foil is an expensive artificial mulch that many people find unattractive. The only place I have ever seen aluminum foil used is in the vegetable garden around warm-season plants.

How to use it. At planting time, place strips of foil on the ground about 2 to 4 inches apart. Plant in rows between the strips. Aluminum foil is not a bad insulator, although most organic mulches are better.

Aluminum foil boosts photosynthesis by reflecting the sun's heat and brilliance — shooting light back up under the leaves of the plant. Aphids and other insects shy away from foil-mulched plants. Aluminum will never rot and should be removed in the fall. If a large amount of aluminum is left in the soil, there is some danger of aluminum toxicity. Foil will break or tear if handled too much or walked on. Aluminized plastic, polyethylene with a shiny metallic coating, is easier to manage than aluminum foil. Aluminum foil can be recycled, a point in its favor over plastic.

Pros. Discourages insects that hide on the undersides of leaves. Can be recycled. Never rots.

Cons. Expensive. Artificial looking. May produce toxicity if left in place for long. Tears if overhandled or walked on.

⟩ BURLAP

Use. Functional

What it is. Burlap is available in natural fiber or synthetic material. Burlap from natural fiber, such as jute, sisal, or hemp, decomposes. The increasingly used synthetic burlap does not break down and should be removed after use.

How to use it. Burlap is effective for preventing erosion on steep slopes and is widely used in grass-seeding operations. After seeding, leave natural fiber burlap on the ground to decay once the grass has grown.

Cons. Because it is so porous that weeds poke right through, it is hard to see how burlap would be of value in the vegetable or flower garden.

⟩ FIBERGLASS

Use. Functional

What it is. Fiberglass consists of woven glass fibers. It is completely fireproof, quite costly, and nonbiodegradable.

When wet, fiberglass insulation absorbs water like a sponge, then compacts. It is valued for its superior insulating quality.

How to use it. Some commercially made fiberglass mats are designed specifically to be used as mulch. Some have holes for plants (and weeds) to grow through.

Cons. Unattractive and costly.

➤ GEOTEXTILES

Use. Functional

What they are. Geotextiles are like fabric, only they're made from synthetic fibers that have been woven, knitted, or matted together. Most geotextiles are made from polypropylene, a petroleum by-product polymer. Some are from polyester, which lasts longer but is more expensive. Geotextiles are generally used for soil stabilization and weed and erosion control on landscape construction sites.

On large and small scales, geotextiles effectively control weeds and conserve soil moisture. Geotextiles are available in quantities and sizes appropriate for gardens of all kinds. They also come as specially designed mats for use around trees, shrubs, and difficult planting spots. Check the Web for suppliers if your local garden centers don't have what you need. Geotextiles are very useful for larger planting areas, walkways, patios, and areas where plants are permanently placed.

How to use them. Clear the area of all weeds first. Then there are two options. If you have precut mats or sheets, just lay the mats down and put plants in the holes. If you're working with loose fabric, roll it out and secure the edges with wire prongs or cover with 1 to 3 inches of organic mulch or stone. Some manufacturers recommend planting first and then laying down the fabric between the rows. Others say to put the cloth down and make slits or Xs where your plants will go. You can decide based on your situation.

Covering geotextiles with mulch — bark, wood chips, crushed stone, or cocoa hulls, for instance — not only looks good, but it also helps them last longer because it protects against UV damage and weather exposure.

Pros. Geotextiles have spaces that allow air and water to pass through. Their dark color blocks light needed for weed germination and growth. Most are treated to be UV resistant.

Cons. They don't contribute anything to the soil. Weeds will still grow in the upper layer of a mulch such as a geotextile. Pull them regularly to keep them from growing into the fabric and creating a new hole for other weeds. It's a good idea to turn cover mulch occasionally to disturb other aspiring seedlings.

⮞ Plastic (Polyethylene)

Use. Functional

What it is. Plastic mulch from polyethylene has spawned a whole new agricultural approach called *plasticulture*. Plasticulture comprises plastic mulches, drip irrigation, row covers, and more, according to the Appropriate Technology Transfer for Rural Areas center in Fayetteville, Arkansas. I won't go into all those subjects but will give you the latest information for earlier and more bountiful vegetable crops.

Plastic mulch is identified by color (black, red, clear, aluminized) and by type (Infrared Transmitting, Selective Reflecting Mulch [SRM-Red]). Details about black and red plastic mulches are included below.

Clear plastic mulch allows soil to warm more than colored plastic, so it's generally used in the cooler regions of the United States, such as New England. Weeds grow under clear mulch, so they must be controlled another way.

Infrared-transmitting (IRT) mulch warms the soil like clear plastic and provides the weed control properties of black mulch. IRT mulch is available in brown or blue-green.

Other colors under study include blue, yellow, gray, and orange. Each color reflects light differently, which affects plant growth and development.

Photodegradable (film) plastic mulch is available. It is like black or clear plastic film but is designed to break down after exposure to the sun so that it doesn't have to be removed later.

Plastic mulch is used mainly to get the earliest crop possible and to prevent water evaporation from the soil. It is effective for warm weather crops and transplants: tomato, pepper, eggplant, okra, muskmelon, watermelon, slicing cucumber, summer squash, and sweet corn. It also works for broccoli, cauliflower, pumpkin, and winter squash as transplants.

How to use it. Plastic mulches come in rolls 3 to 5 feet wide. There are two mulching methods: Lay plastic over the soil bed between the plant rows or lay it over the entire bed and cut holes in it to place plants. To be most effective, plastic mulch must be in contact with the soil.

One way to use landscape fabrics is to lay the fabric first, hold it in place with wire prongs, and put plants in place through slits cut in the fabric. Then cover the fabric with an organic mulch.

Certainly remove all weeds before mulching. It's also best to water the area well before applying the plastic, although walking on wet soil compacts it.

Pros. Plastic mulch has been shown to produce earlier and higher-yielding crops, conserve water, warm the soil, reduce erosion, and reduce weeds. Some types control certain insects: Silver-surfaced plastic repels some aphids. One study found red plastic reduced the nematode population under a tomato crop.

Plastic of any color practically eliminates moisture evaporation. Water condenses on the underside and drips back into the soil. This also tends to keep the seedbed in a friable condition.

Cons. Since it prevents moisture evaporation, plastic also prevents water from penetrating. You will have to take special care to water your plants. Some people install irrigation systems above or soaker hoses under the mulch.

Plastic mulch doesn't allow the soil to breathe, which can lead to some serious disease problems in ornamental plantings. Tree and shrub roots may suffer from the lack of oxygen.

▷ BLACK PLASTIC

Use. Functional

What it is. Black plastic mulch is probably most commonly used in vegetable production and vegetable gardens. Because no light penetrates its opaque surface, *no* weeds can grow beneath it. It reduces soil water loss, increases soil temperature, and improves vegetable yield. Black plastic has long been applied under wood chips or stone to reduce maintenance and retain soil moisture.

Embossed black plastic film has a diamond-shaped pattern to keep the mulch fitted tightly to the bed. Air pockets act as insulation, reducing heat transfer.

How to use it. In some gardens, rows covered with plastic are alternated with bare ground. Most folks who use it lay the plastic before they plant, being sure the soil is fairly moist first. Be certain, if you try plastic mulching, to weight it down properly and to cover all the edges with dirt so the wind can't get under it and blow it away. Cut round, X- or T-shaped holes in the plastic film so plants can grow up and water can go down.

LAYING BLACK PLASTIC MULCH

A

B

Lay the plastic before you plant, making sure the soil is fairly moist (A).

Cut round, X-shaped, or T-shaped holes in the film for plants to grow through and for water to go down.

C

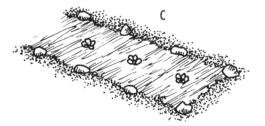

Weight the plastic down properly and cover all edges with dirt so the wind can't get under it and blow it away (C).

⟫ RED PLASTIC

Use. Functional

What it is. Red plastic mulch is Selective Reflecting Mulch (SRM-Red), a new material that performs like black mulch. It warms the soil, controls weeds, and conserves moisture. Why choose red over black? That depends on the crop and your pocketbook. USDA tests show SRM-Red increases tomato production from 12 to 20 percent compared to black plastic mulch. On the other hand, the University of California in Fresno found that red plastic mulch didn't increase strawberry yields compared to black plastic. Runners grew under the red mulch, sapping energy from the main plants.

Red mulch reflects infrared light up into the plant. According to *Science News,* when a tomato plant's pigments detect a lot of infrared, the plant "thinks" that it may be crowded out by competing vegetation. The tomato plant responds aggressively by growing more rapidly.

Red plastic mulch also seems to thwart nematodes under tomatoes. In field studies in Florence, South Carolina, scientists say red-mulched plants grown in nematode-infested soil produced double the tomatoes from plants grown with traditional black plastic mulch. Although they're not sure why, scientists speculate that the red-mulched tomato puts its energy into aboveground growth at the expense of its root system, the nematode's food supply.

A DIFFERENCE OF OPINION

Studies at the University of New Hampshire show that black plastic's dark color absorbs the sun's heat, causing the soil temperature to rise anywhere from 3 to 7°F on a sunny day. Authorities at the University of Vermont, on the other hand, have argued that the heat is given off to the atmosphere above the plastic because a layer of air — which inevitably winds up under the plastic unless you take special precautions to keep it out — acts as insulation.

➤ PYROPHYLLITE

Uses. Decorative and functional

What it is. Pyrophyllite is calcine clay particles, which can be purchased in a fine-grained sand or in 1- to 1½-inch chunks. It's composed of 100-percent-pure, inorganic, inert, nonflammable prophyllite absorbent that's processed at high temperatures to ensure stability and sterility. Calcine clay should be considered a more or less permanent mulch. It is about as decorative as adobe. If you really like adobe, consider buying some; otherwise buy gravel.

Cons. Pyrophyllite absorbs much water, resulting in less for plants.

➤ STONE

Uses. Decorative and functional

What it is. Stone includes gravel, shale, crushed marble or limestone, even volcanic rocks and flagstones. It is one of the most decorative mulches. Stone is used mostly for ornamental landscape beds and around trees and shrubs. It can be effective and striking in a well-tended rose garden. As with all mulches, keep stone from touching the plant stem. Its weight and sharp edges can damage a tender stem, as well as a heavy tree trunk and any extruding roots.

Conkilite is a trade name for lime or marble pebbles that come in small, medium, or large sizes. As advertised, this gives a formalized appearance when it is used as a mulch, but the manufacturer recommends using 8 pounds per square foot!

Pros. Stone retains heat from the sun, so it will warm the soil under it well into a cool evening. It's water permeable.

Stone is available in all sorts of textures and colors. It is permanent and low maintenance in ornamental beds. A few trace elements might leach out of a stone mulch over a period of years, but unless you use limestone, it probably won't dissolve noticeably in your lifetime. If you do use limestone chips, keep in mind that these will raise soil pH and should not be spread around acid-loving plants.

Stone mulches clearly won't be blown around by the wind, mat down in the rain, or tie up soil nitrogen.

Cons. Stone isn't cheap. It is heavy to transport and exhausting to apply; consider hiring a contractor to do the hard work. Weeds find their way through crushed stone pretty easily unless the stone is underlaid with geotextiles or plastic.

Stone is highly impractical for the vegetable gardener. Use it where you are sure you will not till.

As stone is a permanent, low-maintenance mulch, about the only concern is picking up a stray stone with the lawn mower and sending it through the front window. For safety's sake, rake the grass near the flowerbed occasionally and put any stones back where they belong.

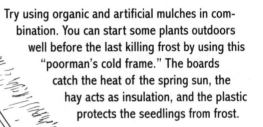

Try using organic and artificial mulches in combination. You can start some plants outdoors well before the last killing frost by using this "poorman's cold frame." The boards catch the heat of the spring sun, the hay acts as insulation, and the plastic protects the seedlings from frost.

❯ VERMICULITE

Use. Functional (indoors)

What it is. Vermiculite (or perlite, which is similar) is a light, mica-like material, so light that it splashes around in a rainstorm.

How to use it. An excellent mulch — one that I heartily recommend for hothouse use. A layer of ½ to 1 inch is enough. Some gardeners claim they have used it successfully in very dry, hot places outside.

Cons. Outdoors, vermiculite is not so good. It's fairly costly and almost totally sterile, which means that it will contribute virtually nothing to the soil in the way of fertilizer.

How Do You Choose?

How do you pick the right mulch for you? While there is no one perfect mulch, there are factors that make one mulch a better choice for a given situation. Specific mulches, as we saw in the previous chapter, have particular advantages and disadvantages. How do you narrow the list? Here are some general guidelines to help you make the best choice.

Cost

Unless you are looking for something terribly exotic, mulch need not be expensive. There is no reason to mortgage the house or skimp on your plant selections to afford the mulch you've always dreamed of. Let's keep things in perspective. Mulching is important but not that important. Shop around a little and price a few types before you decide.

Availability

The availability of a mulch often determines the cost. The laws of supply and demand apply to everything, including mulch. What is plentiful and available is probably cheap — in some instances even free. Check with local municipalities, utility companies, and lumberyards. Many will give away composted leaves or wood chips to someone willing to cart them away. Perhaps a processing plant nearby has excess buckwheat hulls or peanut shells. It pays to check with one or two garden clubs in your area. They often have excellent sources for mulching materials.

Ease of Application

In all fairness, if you plan to mulch on a large scale, you may be doing a fair amount of initial work. On the other hand, you don't want to be a slave to mulching. For an established bed full of trees and shrubs, you probably won't want to slit dozens of holes in landscape fabric or black plastic to cover it. You might not want to hassle with the weight and bulk of crushed stone to mulch a small garden path. Pick a mulch you can handle without having to recruit all the kids from the neighborhood to help you haul it around.

Appearance

Speaking of the neighborhood, try to pick a mulch that won't cause people to whisper behind your back. Experimentation is fine, but try not to offend anyone. Get a peek at what you're thinking of buying, then visualize how it is going to look in your garden. Will those bright red lava rocks go with the rest of the colors in your garden? Black plastic and straw are popular in vegetable gardens but may not look attractive in the peony bed. Eye appeal is a highly personal consideration but definitely worth thinking about.

Water Retention/Penetration

Certainly, you'll want the rainwater to soak down to your plant roots, but permeability isn't as important when you're mulching a pathway. Assess your situation and choose accordingly. The same is true with air exchange. Plastics won't let air in or out, so they can suffocate plants. If, however, your primary concern is weed control, maybe that's acceptable.

Lasting Qualities

In a vegetable garden, you usually turn the mulch into the ground at the end of the season. Chances are you'll want to pick a mulch that decomposes quickly. Conversely, mineral mulches, like gravel and crushed stone, will last for an incredibly long time with a minimal amount of bother. Remember, fine or chopped mulches rot faster, while coarser mulches tend to hang around longer and demand less maintenance.

Staying Power

Obviously, you don't want to spend your Saturday afternoons chasing mulch around the yard. If you live on a windy hill, lightweight mulches like straw or buckwheat hulls are unsatisfactory. Paper or plastic mulches need to be anchored with pegs, stones, or something else. Small, fine bark chips can wash away with the first heavy rainfall on even the slightest incline.

Odor

Not a pleasant topic, I know, but odor does need to be discussed. Manure and poultry litter have their strong points, and often smell is one of them. Sometimes the smell is more than strong — it's overwhelming! Grass clippings can also literally raise a stink. Some people even object to the smell of chocolate given off by cocoa hulls. Keep this in mind when selecting your mulch.

POP ART FOR THE GARDEN

My friend Ted Flanagan, agronomist and vegetable expert at the University of Vermont in Burlington, tells me that his father is probably the best mulching-material scrounger in all the world. "My father will mulch with anything!" he says. But I can't help wondering whether the elder Flanagan isn't second to his son in mulching inventiveness.

Ted has a marvelous collection of mulches, neatly displayed in shoeboxes with impressive engraved plastic labels on them. The collection includes rotting boards, old cedar shingles, paper bags, wrapping paper, paper towels, paper napkins, magazines, underlayment paper, corrugated cardboard (in rolls as well as in strips), shirt cardboards, stump chippings (which he distinguishes somehow from other wood chips), algae (from Lake Champlain, I think), dried silage (which seems to have distinct disadvantages), and a license plate (1968 Vermont registration #1045). Can you think of anything he's left out? What would a psychologist say of a garden mulched with Flanagan pop art?

Quick-Reference Mulch Chart

MATERIAL	APPEARANCE	INSULATION VALUE	RELATIVE COST	THICKNESS	WEED CONTROL
Aluminum foil	Poor	Fair; reflects heat	Very high	1 layer	Good
Asphalt	Poor	Fair	High	½–1 in.	Fair
Bark, mixed	Good	Good	Moderate	2–4 in.	Good
Bark, redwood	Excellent	Good	High	2–4 in.	Fair
Buckwheat hulls	Good	Good	High	1–1½ in.	Good; may sprout
Burlap, natural	Poor	Fair	Moderate	1 layer or more	Poor
Burlap, synthetic	Poor	Fair	Moderate	1 layer or more	Poor
Cocoa hulls	Good–excellent	Good; absorbs heat from sun	High in most areas	1 in.	Good
Coffee grounds	Good	Fair	Low but not plentiful	Never more than 1 in.	Good
Compost	Fair	Good	High; supply usually limited	1–3 in.	Good
Cork, ground	Fair–good	Excellent	High	1–2 in.	Good
Corncobs, ground	Good	Good	Low in Midwest	2–3 in.	Excellent
Cottonseed hulls	Good	Good	Low in the South	1–2 in.	Good

WATER PENETRATION	MOISTURE RETENTION	DECOMPOSITION SPEED	COMMENTS
Poor, unless perforated	Excellent	No decomposition	Aphids shy away from foil-mulched plants. Should be removed and recycled.
Fair	Fair-good	Decomposes in about 1 year	Complicated for home gardener to apply.
Good	Good	Shredded bark decomposes slowly unless composted before use; nuggets deplete soil of nitrogen and take longer to break down	Refresh annually but don't overmulch. Replace every two years if necessary. Dry bark is light and easy to lift with a garden fork. Nuggets require a shovel.
Fair; repels water in some places	Fair	Very slow; add nitrogen to application	Earthworms avoid redwood. May act as an insect repellent.
Excellent	Fair	Slow	Easy to handle. May be blown around in high wind or splashed by rain.
Excellent	Fair	Slow	Excellent for preventing erosion on slopes. New grass grows right through it.
Fair	Fair	No decomposition	Should be removed after use.
Good, unless allowed to mat	Good	Slow; adds nitrogen to soil	Sawdust can be added to improve texture and increase water retention. May develop mold. Has chocolatey smell.
Fair; may cake	Good	Fairly rapid	Use carefully. May prevent ventilation. Best used in container gardens.
Good if well rotted	Good	Rapid; adds nutrients	Partially decomposed compost is an excellent feeding mulch.
Good	Good	Very slow; has little effect on soil nitrogen	Odorless. Stays in place nicely once it has been soaked.
Fair; should be well soaked before applying	Excellent	Nitrogen fertilizer should be added	Avoid close contact with stems of plants because of heat generation.
Good	Good	Fairly rapid	Will blow in wind. Has fertilizer value similar to cottonseed meal.

MATERIAL	APPEARANCE	INSULATION VALUE	RELATIVE COST	THICKNESS	WEED CONTROL
Cranberry vines	Good	Fair	Low in some areas	3–4 in., 2 in. if chopped	Fair–good
Eucalyptus mulch	Good–excellent	Good	High–moderate	2–4 in.	Good
Evergreen boughs	Poor	Good; recommended for wind protection	Low	1 to several layers	Fair
Felt paper (tar paper)	Poor	Good; absorbs heat from sun	High	1 layer	Excellent
Fiberglass	Poor	Excellent	High	3½–6 in.	Excellent
Geotextiles	Poor, without a cover mulch	Poor	High	Single layer	Good
Grass clippings	Poor if not dried. Can have unpleasant odor	Good	Low	1 in. maximum	Fair
Green living ground covers	Excellent	Fair	Moderate	1 layer	Fair
Green manure (cover crops)	Fair	Good once there is a heavy sod	Low	Allow to grow to full height	Good
Hay	Poor, unless chopped	Good	Low, if spoiled	6–8 in., 2–3 in. if chopped	Good
Hops, spent	Fair	Fair; heats up when wet	Low where available	1–3 in.	Good
Leaf mold	Fair	Good	Low	1½ in.	Fair–good
Leaves	Fair	Good	Low	4–6 in.	Good
Licorice root	Good–excellent	Good	Moderate–high	2–4 in.	Good

WATER PENETRATION	MOISTURE RETENTION	DECOMPOSITION SPEED	COMMENTS
Good	Good	Fairly rapid	Excellent winter cover mulch. Pea vines have similar characteristics.
Good	Good	Slow	Refresh yearly as with bark mulch. Reapply as necessary.
Good	Fair	Slow	Good for erosion control. Should be removed from perennials in spring.
Poor, unless perforated	Good	Extremely slow if at all	Difficult to manage, tears. Must be carefully weighted and removed each fall.
Fair; will get soggy and mat	Good	No decomposition	Unpleasant to handle. Totally fireproof. Mats are better than building insulation.
Fair	Good	Rapid with exposure to sunlight; slower with use of cover mulch	Use of a cover mulch highly recommended.
Good if not matted	Fair	Rapid; green grass adds nitrogen	Can be mixed with peat moss. After drying can be spread thinly around young plants.
Good	Good	Will live from one year to the next	Includes myrtle, pachysandra, etc. Use where you are not going to walk.
Good	Good	Decomposing legumes and cover crops are rich in nitrogen	Should be harvested or tilled directly into the soil.
Good	Good	Rapid; adds nitrogen	Second- or third-growth hay that has not gone to seed is ideal.
Good	Good	Slow; rich in nitrogen and other nutrients	Avoid close contact with trunks and stems because of heating.
Fair; prevents percolation if too thick	Good	Rapid	An excellent feeding mulch. Use like compost.
Fair; likely to mat	Good	Fairly slow; adds nitrogen	Contributes many valuable nutrients. Can be chopped and mixed with other things.
Good; fluff occasionally to break crust	Good	Faster than shredded bark	Use like shredded bark. Regional. May be on sale in spring.

Quick-Reference Mulch Chart (continued)

MATERIAL	APPEARANCE	INSULATION VALUE	RELATIVE COST	THICKNESS	WEED CONTROL
Manure	Poor–fair	Good	Moderate–high	As thick as supply allows	Fair
Melaleuca tree	Good–fair	Good	Moderate–low where available	2–4 in.	Good
Muck	Poor	Fair	Moderate	1–2 in.	Fair
Oak leaf mulch	Good	Good	Low	2–4 in.	Good
Oyster shells, ground	Good	Fair	High	1–2 in.	Fair
Paper	Poor; can be covered with soil	Fair	Low, but specialized mulch paper is expensive	1 to several layers	Good
Paper pulp	Poor	Fair	Moderate	½ in.	Fair
Peanut hulls	Good	Good	Low where plentiful	1–2 in.	Good
Peat moss	Good	Good	Moderate–high	1 in.	Good
Pine needles	Good–excellent	Good	Low	1–1½ in.	Good
Plastic	Poor, but can be covered	Fair; some colors absorb heat	Moderate–high	1–6 mil.	Excellent
Poultry litter	Poor	Fair	Low–moderate	½ in.	Fair
Processed sludge	Poor	Fair	Low–free	2–3 in.	Variable

WATER PENETRATION	MOISTURE RETENTION	DECOMPOSITION SPEED	COMMENTS
Fair–good	Good	Rapid; adds nitrogen; packaged mixes may have harmful salts	Should be at least partially rotted. Supplies many nutrients.
Good	Good	Slow	Use like shredded bark. Regional availability.
Good, but will splash and wash away	Fair	Rapid	Very fertile. Can be mixed with other materials to improve texture.
Good	Good	Slow	Recommended for acid-soil plants. Has only slight influence on soil pH.
Good	Good	Slow	Works like lime. Will raise soil pH.
Poor, unless perforated	Good	Slow, unless designed to be biodegradable	Can be shredded and used effectively.
Fair	Good	Rapid, nitrogen rich as side-dressing	Requires special equipment. Useful in deep-planting operations. Good way to recycle.
Good	Good	Rapid; adds nitrogen	Can be mixed with other material for superior appearance. Might splash in rain.
Poor; absorbs much water	Poor; draws moisture from soil	Very slow	Adds little or no nutrients to soil. Valuable only as a soil conditioner.
Excellent	Good	Slow; very little earthworm activity	Often used with acid-soil plants, but can be used elsewhere.
Poor, unless perforated	Excellent	No decomposition	Contributes nothing to the soil. Must be handled twice a year. Various colors available.
Good	Fair	Very rapid; adds nitrogen	Should not be used unless mixed with dry material. Excellent fertilizer.
Good	Good	Rapid–slow, depending on mix	Results will vary according to sludge/wood chips mix. Can be strong, so try on a few plants before using on whole garden or woody plants bed.

Quick-Reference Mulch Chart (continued)

MATERIAL	APPEARANCE	INSULATION VALUE	RELATIVE COST	THICKNESS	WEED CONTROL
Pyrophyllite	Fair	Fair	High	1–3 in.	Fair
Rice hulls	Good	Fair	Moderate where available	1–2 in.	Fair
Salt hay	Good	Good	Moderate, unless you gather it yourself	3–6 in.	Good; contains no seed
Sawdust	Fair–good	Good	Low	1–1½ in.	Good
Seaweed (kelp)	Poor	Good; recommended as a winter mulch	Low in coastal areas	4–6 in.	Excellent
Shredded wood waste	Excellent	Fair	Low–moderate where available	2–4 in.	Fair
Stone	Excellent	Good; dark stone retains heat, light stone reflects	High	2–4 in.	Fair, except shale
Straw	Fair, unless chopped	Good	Low–moderate	6–8 in., 1–2 in. if chopped	Good; avoid oat straw for weed control
Sugarcane (bagasse)	Poor–fair	Good	Moderate	2–3 in.	Good
Vermiculite	Excellent	Excellent	High	½ in.	Good
Walnut shells	Excellent	Good	Low where plentiful	1–2 in.	Good
Wood chips	Good	Good	Moderate	2–4 in.	Good
Wood shavings	Fair	Fair	Low	2–3 in.	Fair

WATER PENETRATION	MOISTURE RETENTION	DECOMPOSITION SPEED	COMMENTS
Good	Fair	Extremely slow	Should be considered a permanent mulch.
Forms water-repelling crust	Fair	Rapid	Limited availability
Good; does not mat	Good	Slow	Can be used year after year. Is pest-free. Good for winter protection.
Fair	Fair	Slow unless weathered; robs soil nitrogen	Has high carbon content. Does not sour soil. Very little earthworm activity.
Fair	Good	Slow; adds nitrogen and potash	Provides sodium, boron, and other trace elements. Excellent for sheet composting.
Good	Good	Slow; add nitrogen to offset nitrogen loss.	Regional availability
Good	Fair	Extremely slow	Should be considered permanent mulch. Contributes some trace elements through leaching.
Good	Good	Fairly slow; nitrogen fertilizer is helpful	Should be seed free if possible. Straw is highly flammable.
Good	Good	Rapid due to sugar content	Needs to be replenished often. Has fairly low pH. Mix with lime.
Good	Good	Extremely slow	Totally sterile. Recommended for hothouse use. Will blow and splash outdoors.
Good	Good	Very slow	Will furnish good trace elements. Resists fire.
Good	Good	Fairly slow; little effect on soil nitrogen	May contain carpenter ants, but does not retain tree diseases.
Good	Fair	Very rapid; will use up soil nitrogen	Hardwood shavings are better than pine or spruce. Chips or sawdust make better mulch.

PART II

Here's How to Mulch

6

TIPS FOR MAKING THE MOST OF MULCH

Now that we know a bit about what to use as mulch, we need to learn how much, where, and when to mulch. I'll make specific recommendations for mulching ornamental plants, vegetables, and fruits a little later. For now let's start with some general tips for getting the most out of your mulch.

MULCHING 101

▶ *Don't try to stretch your mulch too far.* It's like trying to paint with a dry brush. The end result isn't worth much. Try to figure out beforehand how much mulch you are going to need. For a 100-square-foot garden, it will take about 1¼ to 1½ cubic yards of shredded bark, leaf mold, or gravel to make a mulch layer 4 inches deep. That's eight to nine wheelbarrows full of mulch. You can't have too much. It's always good to have extra mulch on hand to replace any that's washed away or decayed, or to cover a newly spaded area. Almost invariably you will end up using more than you thought you would. And you can always stockpile what's not used right away.

▶ *The thickness of your mulch depends on the material you use.* Usually the finer the material, the thinner the layer. Mulch depth can vary from ½ inch for small particles like coffee grounds to 12 inches for bulky stuff like coarse straw.

▶ *Remember that plant roots need to breathe.* Air is one of the vital elements in any good soil structure; 50 percent air and 50 percent solid material is a healthy mix. Soil that is too compact has little or no air. One benefit of mulching, as you'll recall, is that it prevents soil compaction.

Don't mulch so deeply that you undo this good by suffocating your plants' roots under too much or very compacted material. Let your soil breathe. Wet leaves that bond together and cake can be impenetrable. Fine mulches, unless they are applied sparingly, can compact and prevent air penetration too.

▶ *Replace old mulch that's become decayed and compacted.* Mulching promotes shallow root growth. Your plants can become like a spoiled child: Because the soil stays relatively moist beneath mulch, roots do not have to grow deep and work hard. They can stay near the surface. This means that once you start mulching, you are

Amount of Organic Material Needed to Cover a 100-Square-Foot Area

INCHES OF ORGANIC MATERIAL	MATERIAL NEEDED TO COVER 100 SQ. FT. 1 cubic yard = 27 cubic feet
6	2 cubic yards
4	35 cubic feet
3	1 cubic yard
2	18 cubic feet
1	9 cubic feet
½	4 cubic feet
¼	2 cubic feet

Source: Joann Gruttardio, Plant Science, Cornell University

- Use material that won't compress and smother the soil.
- Apply 2 to 4 inches over the root zone.
- NEVER allow any mulch to contact the plant stem.

committed to maintaining it. If you change your mind and remove the mulch in midsummer, your plants may quickly turn crispy and die from lack of water.

▶ *Fluff mulch with your hands or a pitchfork once in a while so it doesn't get too packed down.* Break up the dry crust so water can filter through. If your mulch starts sprouting — perhaps because you have used oat straw or hay with lots of seeds or buckwheat hulls, which might contain a seed or two — flip the mulch upside down on top of the unwanted seedlings to choke them off.

CHOICES, CHOICES, CHOICES

▶ *Refresh or renew mulches in ornamental beds and around shrubs and trees.* Using the same type of mulch in these plantings every season is fine, especially as you'll probably just refresh what's already there. To perk up tired-looking decorative mulch, sometimes just raking will bring larger, more colorful material to the surface. If that isn't enough, you can add new mulch, but remember to remove as much as you replace. Keep the mulch layer 2 to 4 inches deep, no thicker for most mulches. (Ruth Stout's hay and straw approach is the exception.)

Heaping new mulch on old isn't a problem in itself. The danger is in overmulching — increasing 3 inches of wood chips to a 6-inch layer, for example. More is not better. Overmulching is likely to kill your plants, maybe not overnight but after a season or two.

▶ *Do not use the same mulch year after year* in your vegetable garden. This advice is based on the same principle that it is not a good idea to plant the same crop in the same place year in and year out.

A good mulching may last for several seasons. When finally it does decompose, it should be replaced by something else. Plants and soil seem to like variety the way you and I do.

▶ *Apply thicker mulches to sandy, gravelly soils and thinner mulches to heavy clay soil.* Avoid mulching at all in low-lying spots — places that are sometimes likely to be "drowned" with water. Although it isn't always necessary, you can remove mulch during a particularly rainy period, if you have time, to prevent the soil from becoming waterlogged.

▶ *Darker mulches like buckwheat hulls and walnut shells absorb heat and warm the soil beneath them. Lighter mulches, such as ground corncobs, reflect light and heat the soil less.* Choose mulch color according to where you live and according to the heat-loving or hardiness characteristics of the plants you are mulching.

IT'S IN THE APPLICATION

▶ *Cultivate around your plant before applying mulch.* This is important if they have been in the ground awhile without mulch. Loosening the surrounding soil and removing any weeds now will pay off later. Be sure to water the plants generously. Spray with kelp solution or spread fertilizer on the soil now, too. Top with the mulch layer, which will help keep the soil underneath moist.

After-the-fact mulching cannot do much good if the ground is dried and baked hard. This little bit of advance preparation shouldn't be too much of a chore, knowing that you won't have to do any more work there for the rest of the season once the mulch is in place.

▶ *Wait to apply your first mulch until after plants started from seed are pretty well established.* Mulch between the rows first, not right on top of where the seeds were planted. You can begin to mulch the seedlings just as soon as they are an inch or two higher than the thickness of the mulch. Leave an unmulched area about 6 inches in diameter around each plant for about two weeks. Later, when the mulch is good and dry, bring it within 2 or 3 inches of the stems.

▶ *Heavy mulch is most effective if applied after a rain shower,* when the ground is moist (but not soaked). If the ground is too dry to start with, it will tend to stay dry for the rest of the summer unless there is a real cloudburst.

▶ *Do not apply wet mulches, like spent hops or new grass clippings, on very hot days.* Be sure that they do not touch plant stems. When the temperature is above 90°F, such mulches, when wet, tend to generate so much heat that they actually can kill plants they touch.

▶ *Peel off "books" or "flakes"* (3- or 4-inch layers) of hay and place them between rows of vegetable plants. This will make a clean path for you to walk on during rainy days and will keep the weeds down. If any weeds come through in force, add more layers.

Books tend to be pretty dense because the hay is so tightly packed by the baling machine. Sometimes it is a good idea to loosen them by pulling the hay apart a little with your hands. This is an especially good idea if you are going to throw them on top of onions or potatoes that you want to grow up through the mulch.

TWO WAYS TO MULCH ROW BEDS

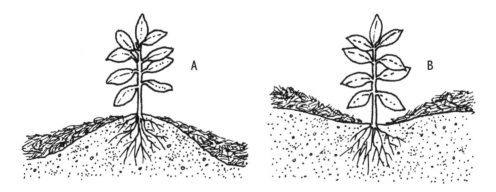

In a rainy year, mound the mulch slightly to encourage some water to run off into the area between rows (A). If it is very dry, make a shallow furrow in the mulch along the row of plants (B). The indentation will tend to collect water, which will seep through the mulch to the plants.

THREE CHEERS FOR MICROBES AND WORMS

▶ *Bacteria and earthworms are strong allies for any gardener.* Without help from lots of microbes in the ground, mulch would never decompose, and the vital elements that are tied up in organic matter would never be released. Worms predigest matter in the soil and liberate chemicals in their castings that plants can use for nourishment. They are also excellent indicators of how useful a material will be as a mulch.

▶ *Earthworms are affected by changes in season and temperature.* They are least active during the hottest months and the coldest months. In the summer they can be coaxed into working harder if you keep enough mulch on the garden to keep the soil moist and cool. In the late fall, earthworms need to be protected from freezing. This is why I recommend mulching annual beds for winter before the ground is frozen hard.

TROUBLESHOOTING WITH ORGANIC MULCHES

▶ *Be alert for signs of nitrogen deficiency* when you use some organic mulches, such as fresh sawdust, wood chips, ground corncobs, and some cereal straws. Bacteria that break down the mulch and turn it into humus require a large amount of nitrogen themselves, so they take nitrogen from the source most available to them: the soil. This, as I have already suggested, makes the plants look yellow and stunted because they are not getting enough nitrogen.

For plants in distress, an immediate spray or watering with kelp solution will help. Follow with an application of alfalfa meal or cottonseed meal scratched gently into soil around the plants. Or use your regular fertilizer as directed. Water well.

▶ *Mold can develop in too moist or shaded organic mulch material.* To get rid of it, turn the mulch regularly. Mold does little harm. In fact, mold is evidence of a healthy decomposition process. It seems to offend the human eye more than it bothers soil or plants.

What's Growing in My Wood Mulch?

Wood and bark landscape mulches can be hosts to several fungi that may look strange but are natural and harmless. Fungi and bacteria are integral to decomposition; they break down wood and bark into humuslike material that plants thrive on.

For instance, mushrooms and toadstools, slime molds, and bird's nest fungus are not harmful to landscape plants or people (unless eaten).

On the other hand, the artillery fungus (a.k.a. sphere thrower or cannon or shotgun fungus) is a real nuisance along the East Coast. An artillery fungus (Sphaerobolus stellatus) is so small that it's easy to miss at first. Clustered, the fungi appear matted and gray or bleached. Up close, they resemble tiny cream or orange-brown cups holding wee black eggs.

Trouble comes during the two to three weeks when the fungi reproduce. When the light, heat, and moisture conditions are just right, they actually shoot these black eggs (sticky spore masses) at light-colored surfaces, such as a white house or bright car. Problem is, this "egg" is like a speck of tar. The sticky, brown and black spore masses are very difficult to remove without damaging the surface of the house or car. One or two spots aren't so noticeable, but en masse they are an unsightly mess. Even if you get them off, the remaining stain requires repainting. In Pennsylvania, insurance companies routinely accept claims to repaint outdoor surfaces and replace the aluminum siding on buildings hit with artillery fungus. In 1999, these fungi caused more than $1,000,000 in damage in the state.

To date, there are no known controls for the artillery fungus. Pennsylvania State University researchers are studying the problem and possible solutions. The Connecticut Agricultural Experiment Station recommends avoidance and prevention. Rake wood chips and bark mulch to disturb the fungus and dry out the mulch. Periodically top off decaying mulch (which contains carbon the fungi use as food) with fresh mulch composed of 90 percent bark. Or replace wood-based mulch with other types, such as black plastic or stone, in areas adjacent to buildings and parking areas.

➤ *Mulches are excellent places for disease spores to overwinter and multiply.* Remove and burn mulching material that you know has become disease infested. Don't till it into the soil. To reduce disease possibilities, don't make mulch from refuse of a plant being protected by mulch. In other words, although chopped pea vines might be an excellent feeding mulch, use them on something other than new pea plants.

TROUBLESHOOTING WITH PLASTIC MULCH

➤ *Disguise plastic mulch by covering it.* If you recognize the advantages of plastic mulch but are offended by the sight of it in your garden, cheer up. Maybe you don't have to look at it. The plastic (or asphalt paper, for that matter) can be buried under a thin layer of something else, like pine needles, crushed stone, wood chips, or hulls of some kind — even dirt!

➤ *Apply water-soluble fertilizer slits in the plastic.* If plants under a plastic mulch show signs of needing side-dressing, dissolve fertilizer in irrigation water that is run through a hose toward the T-shaped slits in the plastic. The stem of the T should point toward the direction the water is coming from.

➤ *Be a creative as well as a practical mulcher.* Experiment, read, and talk to your neighbors. Use your tiller and your chopper, if you have them — even your rotary lawn mower — to help you try out new materials and techniques that the "armchair experts" have not even thought of yet. It is everyday gardeners — sometimes only moderately experienced ones who are not yet set in their methods — who learn the most and can teach us much about gardening.

7

HERE'S HOW WITH ORNAMENTALS

Ornamental plants give beauty to our landscapes. They are the trees, shrubs, perennials, annuals, and bulbs cultivated for their visual appeal around our homes and businesses. Every year homeowners spend millions of dollars to add height, variety, texture, and color to their front and back yards. Mulching is a simple way to help protect and enhance that investment.

Mulching is an integral part of landscaping for several reasons. A richly textured, attractive mulch adds a professional touch to any ornamental bed. Plants can shine as stars while the earthy mulch provides a complementary background. Mulching an ornamental bed conserves water, controls weeds, mediates soil temperature, and stops erosion. Healthy ornamentals improve a property's value. All this makes it easier for you to enjoy more of your time at home.

With high water costs and frequent drought conditions nationwide, mulching is sensible, cost effective, and environmentally sound. As interest and activity in home landscaping climbs, so does the demand for water to keep the plants alive. Without mulch a large portion of this water, some say as much as half, simply evaporates into thin air.

Plants suffer without enough water. A fluctuating water supply stresses them, making them vulnerable to insects and diseases. By conserving water and regulating soil temperature, mulch helps to keep your trees, shrubs, and perennial beds healthy and lush. Also, an organic mulch decays to feed your plants naturally, encouraging worms and microbes who'll do the underground work for you.

As most landscape plantings are perennial in nature, you can use more permanent mulching techniques and materials. It's worth the time and effort to lay down a landscape fabric and cover it with lava rocks if you won't have to hassle with removing it in the fall.

Mulch for landscaping, be it for a single tree or a handsome mixed bed of perennials, shrubs, and annuals, should appeal to the eye. Decorative mulches include shredded barks, stones, wood chips, cocoa hulls, and licorice root. Ground covers such as perennial vinca and pachysandra can act as excellent living mulch, keeping weeds at bay and soil in place in difficult or large areas.

Geotextile fabric topped with shredded bark, natural or colored wood chips, or stone is a popular landscape mulch. Redwood chips over landscape fabric is a good way to add color.

The basics of mulching apply to ornamental use, just as they do for vegetable gardens. Choose your mulch thoughtfully. Before applying any mulch, water the ground well and remove all weeds. Fertilize your plants according to package directions. Apply mulch evenly as if it were a blanket, 2 to 4 inches deep, depending on your mulch and the soil conditions. Don't place mulch against any living stems, trunks, or branches.

To refresh old mulch, give it a light raking to fluff it up, renew the color, and break through any crust. If that doesn't do the trick, remove an inch or two of the organic mulch (wood chips, bark). Then top with new mulch, adding about as much as you removed. Keep mulch in the 2 to 4 inch range. With mulch, more is not always better. Overmulching can be fatal.

TREES

Probably the number one cause of death for newly planted trees and shrubs is the lack of adequate water. We already know that mulch can help solve that problem. Mulching around the tree base also reduces the incidence of mower blight, a.k.a. lawn mower damage, a leading cause of tree death. You know how it is. You're cruising along on your riding mower and cut it just a bit too close to the honey locust tree. Off flies a chunk of bark. While one or two of these weekend collisions won't usually knock a tree out, enough of these bumps and bruises will damage the cambium and the tree will die. Not only that, open wounds in the bark can expose a plant to a number of disease and insect problems.

A good covering of mulch, 3 to 4 inches deep, right after planting will go a long way toward protecting the base of your trees. Before mulching a new transplant, clear away weeds and grasses from the soil surrounding the trunk. A circle 3 to 5 feet wide is a good start. Water generously. Then mulch that cleared area to suppress weeds and grass and help you resist the urge to mow right up to the trunk.

For mulching under established trees, experts recommend clearing weeds and grasses to the tree's drip line. That means beneath the tree's canopy, the shady area under the tree. If that's too overwhelming, clear as large an area as you can. Something is better than nothing.

Next, apply organic fertilizer as directed and water the area well. Top with 3 to 4 inches of organic mulch. And stand back!

A work-saving alternative when temperatures drop in the fall is to spread fresh wood chips out to the drip line. They'll do double duty. The heat from their decay will kill grass under the tree canopy and they'll be acting as mulch, too!

Organic mulches like wood chips, shredded bark or nuggets, cocoa hulls, pine needles, root mulch, leaf mold, and shredded leaves are all smart choices for mulching trees. They decompose, adding to the soil nutrients that are easily depleted by all the tree's shallow

Don't succumb to the common practice of building a volcano of mulch up around any tree or shrub. If you do, you might as well say last rites for your plant. Dark, moist mulch right against bark and branch is the perfect place for insects, diseases, rot, and gnawing critters to feast.

Think "blanket of mulch" instead. Start spreading mulch at least 6 inches beyond the tree trunk or shrub base. Apply an even mulch layer, 2 to 4 inches deep, over the entire bed or tree pit, or beneath a shrub. This mulch blanket will smother weeds and allow water to seep evenly into the soil.

feeder roots. Crushed stone, marble chips, and gravel are fine, but they won't enrich the soil and may be less attractive. Be careful when applying any rock-type mulches around woody plants. Rock mulches can do serious damage to woody plants if they hit the base of the tree. Remember to keep all types of mulch at least 6 inches from the tree trunk.

SHRUBS

To mulch shrubs, follow the basic mulching guidelines. Remove as many weeds and grass clumps as possible, especially in the shady area under the shrub's branches. Apply fertilizer if needed and according to package directions. Water well. Then apply your mulch of choice in an even 2- to 4-inch blanket over the root area. Remember, an organic mulch such as leaf mold or shredded bark will feed your plants for many months to come. Avoid having mulch in direct contact with the shrub's base and branches.

Rhododendrons and Azaleas

There seem to be two shrubs that give people fits when it comes to mulching: rhododendrons and roses. I can understand that roses cause problems because of their demand for winter protection, but I'm not sure why rhododendrons do. I guess it's because we grow rhododendrons and azaleas for their spectacular bloom and when we don't get one, we want to find something to blame. Often, we blame the mulch.

Unmulched or undermulched rhododendrons and azaleas may suffer from chlorosis, weak and underdeveloped leaves, or even death. These plants cannot tolerate hot, dry soil. Their shallow feeding roots are severely injured under these conditions, and the plant has trouble putting out healthy leaves, never mind spectacular blooms. Mulching can help cool the roots and hold the moisture.

In addition, as mostly evergreen plants that carry their leaves all winter, they continually lose water to the air. If soil moisture is inadequate, the plant will lose water faster than it can replace it. The end result will be brown, scorched foliage, which in extreme cases may just give up the ghost and drop off. By watering the ground well and mulching rhododendrons in the fall, you can ensure an ample moisture supply and insulate the soil from sudden temperature changes.

Rhododendrons and azaleas both prefer acidic soils, and your mulch selection can play a part. I suggest you choose one of the organic mulches, like shredded leaves or pine needles. A dry mulch of shredded leaves (especially oak leaves), spread 10 to 12 inches deep, can be laid down at planting (remember, these will decompose quickly to give you a 3- or 4-inch layer). A 2- or 3-inch layer of pine needles will also do the trick, as will wood chips or sawdust, if sufficiently weathered.

If you use one of these mulches, water your rhododendrons following a fertilizer schedule, and still have an unhealthy-looking plant, something else is going on. Maybe you have an insect or disease problem or grew the wrong variety for your area.

MIXED BEDS OF PERENNIALS AND ANNUALS

Decorative organic mulch on a flower bed has multiple benefits:
- It adds the finishing touch.
- It conserves water.
- It controls weeds.
- It moderates soil temperature.
- As it decays, it adds nutrients to the soil.

What more could you ask for? The organic mulch you apply this spring will turn to fertilizer for next spring's growth. I like layering first with 2 inches of leaf mold and topping that with 2 inches of a dark, shredded bark mulch. A mulched, well-fed perennial bed only improves with age. And each year you need to add less mulch!

A New Bed

Mulching a new mixed bed of perennials and annuals is easy. Put in the plants. Water generously and fertilize as needed. Carefully shovel mulch around the new transplants, making sure not to allow mulch to rest against the stems or on the crowns. Mulch on crowns and against stems invites rot, disease, and insect damage. Spread the mulch until you get an even blanket of material about 3 to 4 inches deep.

If your plants are small, such as young annuals, 2 inches of mulch outside them is fine. If you've grouped annuals close together, don't sprinkle mulch between the flowers. Just start mulching an inch or two outside the group.

Remember: One of your major interests is weed control. A deeper mulch layer is best where weeds might be tempted.

FOR THE BEST OF ALL MULCH WORLDS

For an attractive landscape that saves money and gives your plants the most nutrition, try a two-layer approach to mulching ornamentals.

1. Apply 1 to 2 inches of leaf mold or chopped leaves.
2. Top with 1 to 2 inches of shredded bark, licorice root, or cocoa hulls.

It'll look great immediately, and even better next season when the leaf mold's fed your plants.

Keep a close eye on your mixed bed for a week or two. If your plants start to turn brown or look wilted, check to make sure mulch isn't in direct contact. If it is, pull it away. It's not that mulch is harmful; it's just that placed too close to stem and leaves, it can stifle airflow, trap moisture, and become home to insects and diseases.

An Established Bed

Mulching an established mixed perennial bed is best done in spring after the soil has warmed and while the plants are filling out and you can move easily through the garden. As perennials return year after year, most will show their heads proudly. Some, like the balloon flower and coreopsis, are slow to emerge, so walk (and mulch) carefully. Also watch for sprouting seeds; they may be more perennials you'll want to move or cultivate in place.

If you've planted in clusters or groups, mulch outside the clusters and cultivate inside. You want your perennials to have as much room to fill in as possible. The ultimate goal is to have a perennial bed full of, well, blooming perennials! Every year your perennials should spread farther and wider so you'll need less and less mulch.

Weed, water well, and fertilize as needed before mulching. If there's mulch from last season, hoe to loosen it before topping off with a new batch.

If you just don't get to mulching early on, anytime is better than no time. Just remember to weed and water well in preparation. Then allow the foliage to dry before shoveling on the mulch. Placing mulch among fully grown perennials takes patience and precision, so give yourself plenty of iced tea breaks. Better you take an occasional rest than end up crushing your favorite veronica underfoot.

Although it's a chore, be sure to go around and move the mulch an inch or two away from the base of each perennial. Otherwise, mulch in their crowns and against stems is likely to cause rot. I have a small warren hoe (an unusually small-sized triangle) that enables me to get at the base of most plants while standing. To reach some, I have to balance between thorny roses and my favorite, fragile Japanese anemones while bending over to move mulch aside with my gloved hand. Ouch!

Winter Mulch

Generally, winter mulching isn't necessary if you mulched in spring. For fall transplants (shrubs and perennials) and late-season divisions, though, a loose winter mulch of evergreen boughs, pine needles, or pine bark chips is excellent extra protection. The same is true for marginally hardy plants and temperamental shrubs. Use a light mulch that won't mat down, resist water, or be too comfortable a home for rodents. Whole leaves, although handy, aren't a good idea; they'll clump, mat, keep water out, and suffocate anything below. Shredded leaves work well, though. Remember to remove the light mulch in spring when you see new sprouts. Keep some boughs on hand in case you need to cover plants quickly as protection from a late frost.

ROSES

Rose mulching offers a shining example of the differences between summer and winter mulches. Summer mulching is done in the spring to control weeds and maintain soil moisture. Winter mulches, put down after the ground has started to cool in the fall, serve to protect the plant from temperature extremes and soil heaving.

Winter Mulching

Just about everyone who grows roses agrees that winter mulching is necessary to protect their plants. They don't always agree on how to do it. There are probably almost as many methods and materials for winterizing roses as there are rose growers. Winter mulching is fairly simple if you remember why you are doing it. Most roses are amazingly hardy. Mulch isn't meant to keep them from freezing: The goal is to maintain constant temperature and avoid freezing and thawing repeatedly.

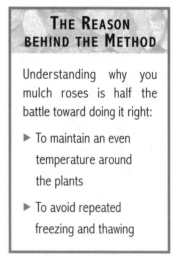

THE REASON BEHIND THE METHOD

Understanding why you mulch roses is half the battle toward doing it right:

▶ To maintain an even temperature around the plants

▶ To avoid repeated freezing and thawing

Here are three methods for mulching roses in winter. Whichever system you select, water the soil well before covering your roses and remove the mulch in the spring before new growth begins. If the mulch is left on until the buds start swelling, it may put the new growth into shock when you uncover it.

1. Mounded soil/mulch method. Probably the most accepted method for winter mulching roses is to take soil or organic mulch from elsewhere in the garden and make a mound of 10 to 12 inches around the base of the rose bush. Do this after the first hard frost. If it's done too early, the roses may be fooled into a late growth spurt, which will delay dormancy and lead to more, not less, winter injury.

Come spring, gently hose away the soil and mulch, being careful not to break off any new sprouting branches.

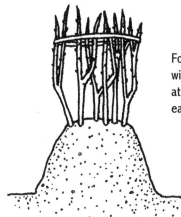

For mulching roses in winter, mound soil/mulch at least 10 inches over each bush.

2. Rose cones/synthetic fiber blankets. Many rose growers combine the mounded soil/mulch method with other techniques. A wide variety of methods and products are available. In areas where the temperature stays well below freezing for most of the season, you will need to provide some additional protection. Some growers lean toward the Styrofoam rose cones that fit around the mounds; others prefer ground corncobs, sawdust, or chopped leaves. Synthetic fiber blankets are an attractive winter protection. Rose cones can overheat during those warm, sunny January thaws. To help keep your roses from "frying," poke a ventilation hole in the top.

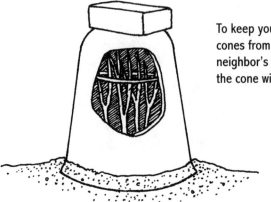

To keep your lightweight rose cones from winding up in your neighbor's yard, weight down the cone with a brick.

3. Wire cages. Wire cages filled with leaves or compost are often used instead of the Styrofoam cones. These cages needn't be stuffed to the gills with leaves. This makes for poor air circulation and may lead to disease problems.

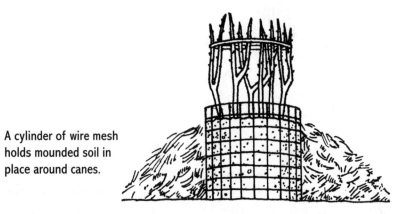

A cylinder of wire mesh holds mounded soil in place around canes.

Summer Mulching

Among true rosarians nothing can stir up such heated arguments as the subject of summer mulching. Some swear summer mulching is a must, while others swear at it. I personally feel it is a good practice.

Antimulchers feel that the threat of insects or diseases being introduced with a mulch outweighs the benefits. Usually these are dedicated growers who have time to pamper and hand-weed their rose beds weekly. I opt for the lower-maintenance, regular-observation method. For amateurs like me, mulching prevents damage to shallow roots during cultivation. I am careful not to mulch right up to the base of my bushes and mindful not to overwater the beds. Moist, damp conditions can foster many rose diseases.

BULBS

Mulching hardy bulbs is not essential. But in a cold-winter area, the insulating value of a nice, thick organic mulch can't be overlooked.

About 2 to 4 inches of shredded leaves, bark nuggets, wood chips, corncobs — just about any mulch that doesn't pack down — is fine for bulbs. Apply mulch after the ground is frozen. Remove in the early spring at the first sign of green sprouts.

8

HERE'S HOW WITH VEGETABLES

The following is a list of annual and perennial vegetables with which I am reasonably familiar. Each item on the list is followed by a discussion of how and when these vegetables might need mulch.

While considering the suggestions made here, keep several things in mind: 1) the general mulching guidelines offered in the earlier chapters, 2) your own experience with a particular vegetable, 3) the climate in your area, and 4) the idiosyncrasies of your garden, such as the soil condition, drainage, the amount of sunlight, and the likelihood of certain pests. As always, I will try to resist telling you what to do and will leave you the burden of deciding whether and how and when to mulch what in your garden.

Just so this doesn't sound like a total cop-out, let me say I think you will find lots of useful information here that you can adapt to your own situation.

Two-Step Mulching

When seeds are first planted,
mulch between rows.

When plants are established, move mulch closer to plants.

Asparagus

If you are just starting a new asparagus bed, mulching probably is not necessary until the second spring — although if you live in a cold place like Vermont or Minnesota, you will want to mulch for winter protection even in the first year. Hay, leaves, straw, old manure, and compost are just a few mulches that are excellent for winter protection of asparagus.

As you know, once a bed has established itself it will continue to produce asparagus for many years. In the spring, there is no need to remove winter mulch. The tips will come right up through the mulch whenever they are ready. Eight inches of hay mulch is not too much for asparagus. Its primary function is weed control, but it may have other fringe benefits.

To extend your asparagus season, divide your bed into two parts in the spring. Mulch half of the bed heavily with a fine material such as cocoa hulls, ground corncobs, chopped leaves, or leaf mold. Leave the other half unmulched until the shoots begin to break through the mulched half. Then mulch where you did not mulch before. Don't worry about weed control with the temporarily unmulched bed — those first asparagus shoots will poke through early in the season, long before any weeds take hold. If you are prompt with your second application of mulch, you'll still have excellent weed control. This technique should extend the asparagus season because the part of the bed that got its start without mulch will begin to bear one or two weeks earlier than the part that started out with mulch.

Beans

You can mulch beans about two or three weeks after planting. Mulching is especially beneficial to beans because it inhibits weed growth. The finer the mulch the better, if you like to plant beans in

---

ADVICE FROM A NEW ENGLAND GARDENER

Arthur Burrage, the well-known New England gardener and writer from Ipswich, Massachusetts, says, "We found that the use of a thick mulch of about four inches of salt marsh straw or salt marsh hay is well worthwhile. It improves the quality, increases the yield, and completely eliminates the need for weeding."

wide rows. Bean roots grow close to the surface, and any deep or extensive cultivation to halt weeds will result in undesirable root pruning of the beans themselves.

I have had trouble growing lima beans. I seem to get a germination rate no better than about 40 percent, and the yield is low, too. If you have luck with them where you are, your lima beans can be mulched with about 3 inches of a light organic material as soon as they are 4 inches high.

I do plant lots of soybeans, in wide rows or just broadcast. Left to their own devices they do just fine, so I don't bother to mulch them, though I'm sure mulch would do no harm. Same with pole beans.

After planting some rows of beans in clear ground in my own garden one year, I poke-planted a wide row of green snap beans with my finger, through a walkway of hay books. I was a man of little faith, so the next day I went back to pull the books apart and loosen the hay a bit. The beans came up through the mulch just as quickly and, apparently, just as easily as those that had no mulch. They grew every bit as strong as, if not stronger than, their unmulched counterparts. In fact, even in extraordinarily wet seasons they look greener and healthier. Possibly this is because, thanks to the mulch, fewer nutrients were leached out of the soil by torrents of rain.

Beets, Rutabaga, and Turnips

Beets like alkaline soil, so it is probably better not to mulch them with pine needles, oak and beech leaves, or peat moss exclusively. Use just about anything else. In fact, adding ground limestone or lime to the soil, or mixing it with the mulch, may be a good idea. Arthur Burrage says that "the use of mulch on the beet bed pays greater dividends than anywhere else on the garden." Ideally, leaves or leaf compost should be spread on beet plots at least once a year and worked into the soil as fertilizer.

A light mulch of grass clippings can be put down right after planting beet seeds, to conserve moisture and prevent the sun from baking the soil hard. As soon as the sprouts appear, pull this mulch back a bit for a while, as beets are highly susceptible to damping off.

As the growing season progresses, increase the thickness of the mulch by adding more layers of straw or hay, and some time after the rows have been thinned tuck it in close to the maturing plants. This procedure seems to work well for turnips and rutabagas, too.

Beets respond badly to boron shortages in the soil. Chopped kelp (seaweed), an excellent organic mulch, can correct this deficiency in a few weeks. Beets also thrive in humus-rich soil, and continuous mulching will contribute to this condition in your soil.

Broccoli

Broccoli can be mulched shortly after the plants have been moved out of the cold frame or greenhouse and set out in the garden. Any nonacidic organic mulch is fine — it will preserve moisture and discourage some insects. Late in the season, because broccoli is naturally frost resistant, the mulch can extend a plant's productive time. Broccoli can stand a maximum of 4 to 6 inches of organic mulch.

Polyethylene works well with broccoli. If you use it, lay the plastic, cut holes, and transplant through the openings. A little fertilizer and lime ahead of time is probably in order.

Cabbage

After your transplants are well established, partially decomposed mulch can be tucked right up under the leaves around your cabbage plants. This may slow their growth somewhat, but they will grow tender, green, and succulent.

According to the Agricultural Experimental Station at the University of Connecticut, an aluminum foil mulch is especially suitable for cabbage. It discourages some disease-carrying aphids.

If you live in a climate that normally experiences mild winters, you might like to plant cabbage seed and cover the beds with a mulch in the late fall — in November or early December. Re-cover the bed with coarser mulch, such as twigs or evergreen boughs, as soon as the seedlings appear. In spring, when you uncover them, you will have some hardy babies for early transplanting.

Cantaloupes and Other Melons

Everyone seems to agree that cantaloupes and other melons need lots of moisture as well as heat, from the time they come up until they are fully grown. Advocates of plastic mulch feel they get an earlier and larger yield by using black polyethylene film. This, they say, is especially helpful when the spring is cool and dry. The film helps to warm the soil, eliminates weeds, and maintains a more constant supply of water to the roots.

A thick organic mulch is designed to do pretty much the same thing. Hay, grass clippings, buckwheat hulls, cocoa shells, and newspapers work fine. It probably is better to stay away from sawdust and leaves. The mulch should be in place before the fruit develops, since handling may damage the tender melons. Once the fruit is formed, it will be resting on a clean carpet of mulch and won't be as prone to rot.

I like to see melon plants maintain contact with the soil because the runners themselves absorb moisture and nourishment from the ground. So I discourage the use of plastics or any organic mulch that the runners can not be tucked under easily. In fact, in a normal year I prefer no mulch at all at least until the fruit has started to form. Then, to keep the fruit clean, I carefully set the melons on top of tin cans. This also makes them sweeter — I don't know why, exactly, but I think it might have something to do with the melons getting more uniform heat. A tin can mulch, you say? How could master mulcher Ted Flanagan have missed that one?

Carrots

Mulch should be used very sparingly on carrots. When you sow carrots, you might want to spread a very thin mulch, say of grass clippings, over the beds to prevent the soil surface from forming a crust that the sprouting seeds can't break through. Water this mulch if you like, but be careful that the tiny seeds don't wash away. When the slender seedlings come up, be sure that the mulch does not interfere with them.

Ground coffee makes a good mulch for carrots, and you can apply it when you sow your seeds. Just mix a packet of seeds with 1 cup of fresh ground coffee and sow as usual. This light mulch seems to discourage wireworms.

Have you tried leaving your carrots in the ground during the early winter months to save storage space in the house? They can be kept there, covered with a heavy mulch to prevent freezing and thawing damage. Once dug up they won't keep long, but many people prefer them to frozen or canned carrots from the supermarket.

Cauliflower

Cauliflower can be mulched in much the same way as broccoli. Mulch right to the lower leaves shortly after transplanting, or lay plastic and plant through it.

Celery

The traditional way to "blanch" celery is with a soil mulch. Earth is pulled around the plants as they get higher, until finally, when the celery is fully grown, the celery rows are about 18 inches high and only the green tops are showing. As a cleaner alternative, try an organic mulch rather than soil to blanch your celery. Chopped leaves are best; whole leaves may dry out and blow away.

Celery that is protected with a deep mulch will produce crisp, tender hearts until Thanksgiving or later. Ideally the heavily mulched rows should be covered with sheet metal, plastic, or some other waterproof material to form a tent; with this protection, the ground stays dry and will not freeze too hard. You will be able to dig celery any time you want it, even in midwinter. Just shovel away some snow, remove the tent, and uncover as much celery as you want to eat. Celery that is protected this way keeps better than in a root cellar.

Corn

Some gardeners, like Ruth Stout, keep a permanent organic mulch on their corn patches. At planting time they just run a straight line with a string and push their corn seeds down through the mulch with their fingers. After the harvest, Mrs. Stout simply breaks the stalks over her foot and throws more hay over the old mulch.

Permanent mulchers argue that crows seem to be nonplussed by the heavy layer of mulch over corn. They often will pull out small corn plants nearly as fast as they show aboveground. If the corn has had a chance to get a good head start under mulch, the plants will yield disappointing results to the average crow, who is after those tender sprouted kernels below the plants.

Here in Vermont, where I worry about soil warmth until as late as early June, I plant corn in the bottom of a furrow and use no mulch for a while. I cover the seed with about an inch of soil — which doesn't begin to fill the furrow — and stretch 12-inch chicken wire over the top of the furrow. The birds are unable to reach the planted kernels or the shoots through the wire. If you have no way to make a furrow (I just use a little furrower that attaches to the back of a rototiller), bend some 24-inch chicken wire down the middle to make an inverted V and form a tent over your row of corn. Be sure to close off the ends, or the birds will get in there and saunter down each row, picking kernels of corn seed out of the ground as they go. Remove the chicken wire tents once plants are 3 inches tall.

According to the old maxim, corn should be "knee high by the Fourth of July." At just about this point, when the corn is "tall enough to shade the ground," it's time to mulch your corn. The stalks have been spaced or thinned carefully so they can be mulched without damage. The wire, of course, long since has been taken up. Use any mulch that will preserve moisture and give the corn an extra boost by adding nutrients to the soil.

Cucumbers

Chopped leaves, leaf mold, straw, and old hay are good for mulching cucumbers. Mulch somehow seems to keep cucumber beetles away. It can be put around the plants when they are about 3 inches high and before the vines really start to extend. Cucumbers, of course, require much moisture, which the mulch will help to retain. Some organic mulches, as you already know, will invite some slugs, snails, diseases, and insects other than the cucumber beetle to your cukes. To be on the safe side, keep the mulch 3 or 4 inches away from the main plant.

Eggplant

Eggplant needs all the warmth it can get. Don't mulch it until after the ground has really had a chance to warm up. Also, avoid disturbing the earth immediately around eggplant. Once the soil is warm enough, mulch will smother most weeds before they grow big enough to be pulled.

The roots of these finicky plants prefer to grow and feed in the top 2 inches of soil. If there is too little moisture there, the leaves turn yellow, become spotted, and drop off; if there is too much, the plant will not bear fruit. Mulch can help to keep a uniform supply of moisture there.

Eggplant is also apt to attract flea beetles. Aluminum, laid temporarily on top of other mulch, has been known to thwart these insects.

Garlic

Garlic can be mulched when the plants are 6 to 8 inches high. Use a fine mulch like hulls, grass clippings, or chopped leaves. For more advice, see the Onions entry.

Kale

Kale is an incredibly hardy vegetable. It can be grown nearly any time of year. A fall or winter crop may be left in the field, covered lightly with something like hay, pea or cranberry vines, or straw. Later in the winter remove the snow (one of the mulches kale seems to like best, by the way) and cut the leaves as you want them. Kale will sometimes keep this way all winter, if it doesn't get smothered by ice after a thaw.

Leeks

Leeks and scallions can be mulched lightly with anything from straw to wood shavings. Just be sure that the mulch does not interfere with the very young seedlings. For more advice, see the Onions entry.

Lettuce

Leaf lettuce does well in semishade and in humus-rich soil. A very coarse mulch such as twigs, rye straw, or even pine boughs can be used in the seedbed. As the leaves grow, move the mulch right up underneath them. This does four things: It holds the soil moisture, keeps the leaves from being splashed with mud, prevents rot, and maintains the cool root run that many plants — especially cold-season vegetables like this — require for optimum production.

You can apply as much as 3 inches of mulch as soon as head lettuce is 3 or 4 inches high and has started to send out its leaves. According to Arthur Burrage, this helps to ensure good plant growth. Every head should mature properly this way, Burrage says: "It has always been a pleasure to look at the lettuce bed. There are rows of perfect heads resting on a light brown carpet of delightful appearance."

Onions

Mulching helps onions. Almost everyone seems to agree on that. Even local folks who hesitate to mulch many things because they understand Vermont's fickle climate will remark, "You can't kill an onion." Onions can and should be mulched during long hot spells. Chopped leaves can be sprinkled among the green shoots even if they are 2 or 3 inches high. Mulched onions will grow slowly and be more succulent than onions grown without mulch. A little more mulch can be added as the tops develop.

Ruth Stout says, "Onion sets may be just scattered around on last year's mulch, then covered with a few inches of loose hay; by this method you can 'plant' a pound of them in a few minutes, and you may do it, if you like, before the ground thaws."

I have planted onion sets several different ways myself:
- Planted in bare ground and left alone
- Planted in bare ground and mulched with finely chopped leaves when the plants are 4 to 6 inches high (this looks most attractive)
- Thrown under about 6 inches of hay mulch

I've noticed that the growth of the onions in bare ground tends to be very slow. And it almost seems that those mulched with the chopped leaves stop growing entirely. But the ones under hay have done well, growing large bottoms. Explain that one to me if you can.

Arthur Burrage uses a slightly modified approach. He puts down 2 to 4 inches of mulch when the onion tops are about 6 inches high. Burrage writes:

> *F*or this mulch we use the remnants of what mulch was used in the bean, corn, and pea area of the previous year. We find that the remnants are broken down into smaller pieces and are easier to handle in rows planted close together than something like fresh straw. The few weeds that grow are easily pulled and the beds stay neat looking all summer. Our experience has been that our troubles, at least as far as onions are concerned, are over for the season. Nothing is left to do except to pick them.

Parsley

In places where winter is not as harsh as in the north, parsley can be protected by mulch throughout the winter. It can be planted in cold frames in August — or even later — covered with hay, left in the frames all winter, and transplanted to the garden in the early spring. Parsley is susceptible to crown rot, so summer mulches should be kept 5 to 6 inches away from the plant.

Parsnips

Parsnips do not grow well in tight, compacted soil: Instead of growing one straight root, they divide into three or four, which makes the root worthless. Mulching can help here by preventing compaction. But parsnips prefer a soil with a pH of about 6.5, so don't use an acidic mulch. Like beets, parsnips will suffer if there is a boron deficiency in your soil. Seaweed has traces of boron and is often recommended for winter protection. Try some on your parsnips.

Most gardeners can eat parsnips from their gardens all winter if they are heaped high with leaves or some other protective mulch as cold weather moves in. They store very well. Don't use them until after the first heavy frost; they won't have reached their peak of quality until then anyway. Most folks think they are best in November and December. Will they survive −30°F? I keep forgetting to ask my mountaintop friend how his fared.

SOME LIKE IT COLD

One winter I had the misfortune to be skiing on a very cold day in January. The temperature at the top of nearby Mt. Mansfield was about −30°F with a high wind. An abominable snowman helped me off the chairlift at the top of the otherwise abandoned mountain. When he spoke through his frosty whiskers, I recognized him as a friendly, lifelong resident of Stowe village, six miles below. "Think this cold'll hurt the parsnips?" he asked. Parsnips do indeed have a cold-hardy reputation.

Peas

It is easy to overdo mulching peas in a cool climate like ours. The soil around peas does need to be cool and damp. In dry soil they will not germinate well, and a large percentage of the seeds will be lost. In late spring around here, I usually don't have any trouble meeting either of these conditions without using mulch.

To grow peas in much warmer places, or to grow pea varieties like Wando later in the summer, mulch with a thin layer of grass clippings, straw, or hay when the seeds are sown. (I broadcast peas in some places and then bury them just under the surface with the rototiller.) As the plants get started, you can increase the mulch to insulate the soil from the atmosphere and the hot sun. This way you can almost assure yourself of a cool, moist root run.

One June, just as I was finishing planting my own peas in the traditional way (in rows without mulch), my wife called me to lunch. I still had a large fistful of seeds in my hand. Indolent fellow that I am (also very hungry, and a little curious, too, if the truth be known), I decided to throw the seeds away instead of putting them carefully back in the bag. With a furtive, sweeping gesture I quickly tossed the evidence of my own wastefulness under the rug of very heavy hay mulch. To my surprise, even though the seeds actually were never planted in the soil, the plants came up en masse and looked healthy and green.

The last time you pick your peas each season, pull up the whole vine before you remove the pods. This should help save your back. The vines should be stacked and saved, too. Chopped or whole, they are a nitrogen-rich mulch that can be used anywhere on the garden, except on other peas.

Peppers

The growing habits of sweet peppers are very much like those of tomatoes. I often plant these two at the same time as companion plants. Early plants respond well to a black paper mulch. This will collect the heat of the day and help maintain a warm soil temperature for a while into the night. Later the paper mulch can be taken off and replaced with an organic mulch, or not replaced at all.

I have learned that pepper plants grown under hay mulch may be stunted and slow to mature. On the other hand, my own pepper plants, which are surrounded with dark, chopped leaf mold mixed with alfalfa meal, are quite a bit ahead of some peppers in other gardens. Peppers and dark-colored mulches seem to go well together.

Potatoes

Potatoes, if you use mulch, don't even need to be planted! As Ruth Stout says, "Many people have discovered that they can lay seed potatoes on last year's mulch, or on the ground or even on sod, cover them with about a foot of loose hay, and later simply pull back the mulch and pick up the new potatoes."

This oversimplification may appear to some as another unfortunate Stoutism, but she is correct in saying that you can grow potatoes "under mulch, in mulch, on top of mulch — almost any way in fact — and get satisfactory results." You can harvest early potatoes from their thick mulch bed and then replace the covering.

Deep mulch also seems to thwart the potato bug, whose larva winters in the soil. Apparently these fellows are reluctant to climb up the potato stem though the thick hay.

Pumpkins

Pumpkins profit from freshly cut hay, composted leaves, straw, and cow manure. Mulch around each hill. As the crop starts to mature, use any coarse mulch that keeps the fruit off the ground.

Radishes

Mulch is not recommended for quick-growing plants like radishes, as there usually is not enough time for mulch to do them any good. For the most part, plants that prefer cool, moist soil respond better to mulches than those that revel in hot sun and dry soil.

Rhubarb

Thick stalks of rhubarb result from continuous heavy feeding. Spread a thick mulch of strawy manure over the bed after the ground freezes in the winter. In the spring, rake the residue aside to allow the ground to warm and the plants to sprout. Then draw the residue, together with a thick new blanket of straw mulch, up around the plants. Hay, leaves, or sawdust also makes excellent mulch for rhubarb.

Spinach and Swiss Chard

Mulching spinach and similar vegetables seems like a waste of time to me since they're such short-season crops, but some say that spinach can be mulched with grass clippings, chopped hay, or ground corncobs and be better for it. Since spinach does not do well in acidic soil, avoid peat moss, oak and beech leaves, pine needles, and sawdust. In any case, I don't advise putting down a summer mulch until the leaves have had a chance to make a good growth.

Squash

Squash can use an extraspecial dose of mulch, especially during hot, dry spells. The mulch, whether it be rotted sawdust, compost, hay, or just leaves, can be as deep as 4 inches. Leave the center open so that some heat can get to the middle of the plant. The mulch over the rest of the patch will preserve moisture and discourage some bugs. I probably don't need to remind you how much space is taken up by squash. Be sure that you have plenty of mulch before you commit yourself. Don't bother mulching winter squash.

THIS SQUASH REALLY ROCKS

Kerr Sparks, a friend of mine, grows beautiful zucchini and acorn squash in a rock mulch — and I mean rocks, not crushed stone. Some of the rocks are 10 to 12 inches in diameter. Kerr's wife and some of his neighbors started worrying about his sanity when he started packing these big stones around his young squash plants. "They didn't do much at first," he says, "but later in the spring when the sun got to the rocks, it was frightening. The plants grew as much as 7 inches in a day!"

He gave me one huge zucchini to try. It was every bit as tender as the young, small zucchini I normally prefer. And the seeds, for some reason, were small, few, and far between. This must have something to do with the fast growth the squash makes as it rests on the warm stones. Don't you have a lot of rocks around your place you've been wondering what to do with? Now you know.

Sweet Potatoes

Sweet potatoes are ravenous feeders and are happiest in plenty of moisture. Compost is an ideal mulch for just these reasons. Old leaves and grass clippings make a good organic side-dressing, as do the old standbys, hay and straw. If you plant sweet potatoes in hills, mulch and fertilize them well, and allow them lots of room to develop.

Tomatoes

Some vegetables such as tomatoes (as well as peppers and corn) need thoroughly warmed soil to encourage ideal growth. A mulch that is applied too early in the spring, before soil temperatures have had a chance to climb a little in frost zone areas, will slow such crops. Generally, in colder climates, tomatoes need less mulch. Dark-colored mulches can help seal in heat and moisture.

Black and red plastic mulches, used in commercial cultivation, are increasingly popular among gardeners who want earlier crops and more fruits and vegetables. Black and red plastic mulches warm the soil so you can start planting earlier and continue harvesting longer. They also conserve moisture and control weeds. They are best applied either before or soon after plants are in the ground.

Red plastic mulch is Selective Reflecting Mulch (SRM-Red), a new material that performs like black mulch. It's more expensive than the black, but USDA tests show it increases tomato production by about 40 percent; it also reduces nematodes (see page 60).

A good time to mulch with other materials is right after the flowers appear. Blossom-end rot can be caused by a variable moisture supply. Mulch keeps a more consistent supply of moisture around the roots of the plants. I have used chopped alfalfa hay, chopped pea vines, chopped leaves, and straw. Early plantings have been mulched with felt paper to keep the soil warm. If you have lots of mulch and few sticks to use as tomato stakes, forget about staking. Let your plants run around freely over the mulch and let the fruit ripen there.

Watermelon

Here is still another plant that should not be mulched until the soil is really warm. How many gallons of water do you suppose there are in one large watermelon? Obviously the melons demand all kinds of soil moisture. The best time to apply mulch is when the soil has been dampened thoroughly. Up to 6 inches of mulch can be spread over the entire patch, if you like, to prevent rot and to keep the fruit dirt free.

9

HERE'S HOW WITH FRUITS

I wish that this chapter could have a title like "Mulching Fruits: A Month-by-Month Calendar." Unfortunately, seasons and climates vary so much throughout North America that such an approach would be inaccurate and confusing to many people. We will have to be content with general descriptions of what to do in spring, summer, autumn, and winter.

SPRING

As the snow starts to melt during those first warm, sunny days of spring, gardeners everywhere start champing at the bit. This is the season for restraint. Because most fruits are perennial plants already in place, it is easy to jump the gun on a day with 60°F temperatures. Think about other things if you can. Try to remind yourself that there aren't many things to worry about in the garden itself just yet. Loosen mulch where it has been crushed by snow, if you like, but don't remove it too early. Spring is a good time to scout around and see what you can scavenge in the way of mulching materials.

Early spring is the time to plow, spade, or rototill winter mulch into seedbeds where you will be planting your annual plants. Don't remulch perennial fruits until at least two weeks after the average date of the last killing frost, whenever that may be where you live. Give the earth plenty of time to warm up.

By mid-April here in Vermont we are just *beginning* to remove winter mulch from the perennials, about three or four weeks after the snow has left our valleys. This date probably will be earlier where you are. Remember: Removing too much mulch from perennial plants too early does *not* help the soil and the roots to warm up. It may warm it for a few hours, but after the next hard freeze and subsequent thaw (and we have plenty of those in late April and May) plants may be frost-heaved right out of the ground and die of root exposure.

Move protective mulch away from plants gradually and let it lie off to the side, but within easy reach. Take off one thin layer at a time, waiting several days before you remove the next layer. This painfully slow process gives your plants a chance to harden.

Josephine Nuese, in her book *The Country Garden* (Scribners, 1970), says,

> **D**on't whip off winter protection until the soil beneath the plant has thawed out. Strong March winds and strong March sun, both dehydrating, can drain the essential moisture which the still frozen roots can't replace. Don't be misled by shallow surface thawing. If you poke down with a stick and can feel ice, leave the mulch.

As much as anything else, mulch should be kept on so the roots and tender shoots won't grow too *soon* and get nipped by frost. If it's possible, remove the final layer of mulch on a cloudy day so that any young shoots that *have* started are not blasted suddenly by brilliant sunshine. Once the winter mulch is off completely, leave it off for several days, or even a couple of weeks, before you start to mulch again.

In the *late* spring start mulching again, to conserve moisture and control weeds before they get a head start. This is a good time to fertilize around fruit trees and berry bushes by adding some sort of feeding mulch, which will contribute humus and nourish the plants. Nitrogen-rich grass clippings usually abound at this time. Use them, but dry them first. Mulch far enough away from your fruit trees — out at least to the drip line (that's the outer perimeter of the tree if you are looking straight down on it) — so you can be sure your mulch is doing some good directly over the tiny feeder roots.

SUMMER

Summer is the time when mulching should start to pay dividends. During hot spells, roots should thrive in the weedless, cool, moist ground under mulch. You do nothing now except have a look every now and again and renew the mulch wherever weeds show signs of getting the upper hand. Pull any weeds that show up.

Be crafty about choosing materials for summer mulching. Because your fruits will not be tilled, it becomes particularly important to encourage earthworms into your perennial beds in order for your soil to get some aeration. Avoid using mulches like sawdust, pine needles, and redwood by-products, because earthworms don't like them. A continuous mulch around thick-stemmed shrubs and trees should be a coarse, heavy material that allows plenty of water through, but that is not going to decay too rapidly (it should last for several years). Topdress through the mulch with fertilizer whenever it seems appropriate.

One thing to look out for: There is danger of crown rot in small fruits — strawberries, for example — during the early summer months. If there have been especially heavy rains, postpone your mulching until the soil no longer is waterlogged. Do not allow mulches — especially peat moss, manure, compost, spent hops, or ground corncobs — to touch the bases of your plants. Leave mulch-free circles around the stems several inches in diameter. The idea here is to permit the soil to stay dry and open to the air around the immediate area of the plant.

Mulch should be maintained in a young or dwarf fruit orchard throughout the summer. Organic gardener and farmer Chuck Pendergast, in his book *Introduction to Organic Gardening* (Nash Publishing, 1971), reports:

> *I*n early fruit orcharding, the practice was to let the trees go to grass. In other words, the land surrounding the trees in an orchard was not cultivated and plant life was allowed to establish itself there. Year after year, this resulted in a gradual building-up of the sod. The more time it has, the tighter sod will become. Eventually there was a conflict between the grasses covering the ground around the trees and the trees, which were being deprived of necessary quantities of water. Hence the practice of keeping the land in an orchard free from growth began.
>
> The immediate results of this practice were favorable. The trees' health and yield improved. . . . As it is hard to prevent cover grasses from becoming detrimental once they become established, mulching is now a widespread practice in orcharding. . . . We've learned smothering and put it to wise use.

AUTUMN

The longer the perennial's roots can stay at work in the fall, the better — up to a point. Late mulching can prolong a plant's growing season because it provides a buffer zone against frost. Roots will continue to grow in soil as long as moisture is still available there. When the soil water freezes and is unavailable to roots, they stop. Increase your mulch volume gradually for a while to insulate the soil and to prevent early freezing of soil moisture.

Once the frost has been on the pumpkin more than a couple of times, your plants probably should be given a hardening-off period similar to the one you gave them in the spring. Remove the mulch gradually until the plants are obviously dormant and the ground is frozen.

By now you should be collecting materials for winter mulching. Maybe you will want to cut evergreen boughs. They do a great job of holding snow (which is a superb mulch) in places where it might otherwise be blown away. After harvest time, push mulch back away from fruit trees, leaving an open space around the trunks. If you anticipate that a winter rodent problem will develop in berry bushes, grapes, or dwarf fruit trees if mulched with seedy materials, don't forget that you can wrap wire mesh, hardware cloth, or plastic protectors around trunks and berry canes.

Fall is the best time to make use of your chopper by grinding up plant residues for future use as mulch. Use your rototiller, if you have one, for sheet-composting leaves between rows. Till in the summer mulch, too.

WINTER

Should winter mulching of perennials be done before or after the ground is frozen? This has been a source of much controversy and confusion in mulching circles. Don't be confused: Remember, this chapter has to do with perennial fruits. Mulch your *annual* beds early — before frost really has settled into the soil — so that earthworms and beneficial microorganisms can stay at work longer during the cold months.

That makes sense for annuals, you might be saying. But what about perennials? Do they need winter mulching?

I *have* made a study of this — a cursory one, at least. I asked the question, "Why does Mother Nature arrange to have her trees drop their leaves, and then later see to it that a heavy blanket of snow insulates the ground even more? Can winter mulching then be a bad thing?"

Some would still argue that a garden should be left naked and exposed for the winter. John and Helen Philbrick have written:

Mulch should not be left on over the winter because it prevents the beneficial action of the frost in the earth. Moisture should not be hindered from 'coming and going' during the seasons of snow and ice. If protective mulch is in such a condition that it will break down during the winter and become part of the topsoil, it may be left. But the home gardener should study this subject carefully and be sure he knows exactly what he is doing and why he is doing it."

I would argue that your garden, especially your perennials, should have winter mulch. Winter mulch keeps winter soil *frozen* — even during thaws. Winter moisture and frost ought to be allowed to penetrate the soil before you lay down a heavy winter mulch. Then, if the mulch keeps the frost in, the plants cannot be "heaved" out of the ground when the soil expands and contracts on alternately freezing and thawing days.

Winter mulch protects perennial foliage from drying winds and too-bright winter sunshine. It prevents the absorption of heat in the spring and doesn't allow anything to grow until after the last killing frost when finally it is removed. The initial question (in case you've forgotten): Should winter mulching of perennials be done before or after the ground is frozen? The answer: after.

Last question: How much winter mulch is enough? I suppose that it is possible to smother plants under too much winter mulch. One approach to the problem might be to find out from your local bureau of the United States Weather Service the average frost depth in your area. Then roughly estimate how deep your plants' roots are. Once you know this, you might find that Dr. D. E. Pfeiffer provides a clue. In John and Helen Philbrick's *Gardening for Health & Nutrition*, he is quoted as saying, "Winter mulch does the same thing that snow does: It insulates the soil to the same depth as the height of the mulch. If there is a three-foot snowfall, the effect of the snow reaches down to a depth of three feet. A mulch acts in the same way . . ." This doesn't mean that you have to mulch to a level equivalent to the bottom of the frost level. That would mean as much as 4 feet of mulch in Vermont! It only means that you should mulch to a height that is a little greater than your perennial plants' roots are deep — that is, if the frost level where you live goes below that point.

HOW WINTER MULCH WORKS

Without mulch. Alternate freezing and thawing can heave plants out of the ground, causing root damage.

With mulch. Evergreen boughs anchor snow and offer fine winter protection for perennial plants.

FRUIT TREES

I am going to cheat a little here and lump all tree fruits together. I couldn't find anything to justify treating peaches differently from pears, or cherries differently from apples. I did find mulching to be highly recommended for fruit trees. As with other plants, mulching will help regulate soil moisture and soil temperature, control weeds, and improve the soil structure. An additional benefit to mulching around your fruit trees is that a nice, soft bed of straw or leaf mulch will cushion fruits that drop from the tree.

One real danger when mulching fruit trees is the threat of rodent damage. Rodents have a particular taste for fruit trees and, as I said earlier, mulched trees are even more enticing. Be sure to leave a space of several inches between your mulch and the base of the tree and use a tree guard.

Straw, hay, grass clippings, and sawdust are excellent choices for fruit trees. These break down relatively fast and have to be replenished. Woody mulches or coarsely ground corncobs, which last anywhere from three to five years, may involve less work. If you decide to use these longer-lasting mulches, don't forget that your trees still should be fertilized once a year or so. Black plastic can also be spread around the base of the trees in the spring to control weeds, but pick it up before late fall to eliminate potential nesting sites for mice.

Organic mulches can be applied to a depth of 6 inches. They will decompose to about half that thickness and you may have to add more. The mulch should be kept at or near that 6-inch depth for good weed control. If it will look all right, apply the mulch out from the tree trunk to slightly beyond the spread of the branches. This gives those falling fruits a larger target and protects more of the root area.

STRAWBERRIES

W. H. Thies says that organic mulching can make the difference between a successful strawberry planting and an abysmal failure. He may be over-dramatizing a little, but mulch can be very helpful. The nicest thing about mulching strawberries is that the mulch keeps the fruit clean.

Strawberries can be mulched right after planting. Chopped hay or straw is most frequently used. Some like to use sawdust or grass clippings. Apply 3 inches of straw and only 1 inch of sawdust or grass. Be careful not to cover the strawberry leaves with the mulch. A lot of folks are using black plastic around their strawberries. Of course, this is better applied before planting.

Winter mulching is essential to successful strawberry growing. It not only prevents heaving, which breaks roots, but protects the vulnerable crown of each plant, which is in real danger in temperatures below 10°F. The plants should be protected by several inches of mulch whenever temperatures stay below 20°F for any extended period of time.

Don't mulch your strawberry plants before that — early mulching can do more harm than not mulching at all. Covering your plants too soon will block sunlight from the leaves and halt photosynthesis. This will prevent the plants from producing and storing enough carbo-hydrates to get through the winter.

Straw is generally the mulch of choice for winter protection, but some work at Cornell University shows that row covers might also do the trick. Marvin Pritts, assistant professor with Cornell University's Pomology Department, explains that row covers have a few advantages over straw: "Unlike straw, they are lightweight, easy to handle, weed-free, and do not delay bloom. Some are even biodegradable. In addition, they allow light to penetrate in the spring, resulting in higher yield."

Pritts recommends removing the row covers before the plants start flowering, or they may block pollination and increase the plants' susceptibility to botrytis fruit rot.

If you use one of the organic mulches, uncover the plants in late spring, when the new growth is about 2 inches long. Again, don't be overanxious. An early spring frost can nip off uncovered strawberry flowers, and you'll end up with fewer berries. As you remove the mulch, put half of it in the pathways between rows and leave the other half for the plants to grow through.

Raspberries and Blackberries

Don't mulch to heavily, or new growth may not be able to push through a thick layer.

Mulch raspberries and blackberries almost immediately after planting to improve yields and lessen cold injury. I use chopped hay or leaves or a combination of the two. Sawdust, wood chips, shavings, dried chopped cornstalks, and poultry litter can also be tried. Apply 3 or 4 inches to the row or over the entire soil surface. Be alert for nitrogen deficiencies.

Blueberries

Mulching blueberries can be a tricky thing. Some argue that they should not be mulched at all unless there is good soil drainage. Overmulching can make blueberries more susceptible to diseases. Other authorities admit that blueberries are apt to ripen later if they are mulched, but claim that higher yield is the end result.

Sawdust and chopped cornstalks are excellent mulches for blueberries. Although some sawdust mulches may make soil slightly more acidic, this would not hurt the blueberries. They seem to do best in a soil with a pH of 4.5 to 5.0, so they should never need lime. This means they can stand a permanent mulch, anywhere from 4 to 6 inches, of pine needles, peat moss, oak leaves, beech leaves, or other mulch that releases acid seepage. Black plastic, neither sweet nor sour, works well on blueberries, too.

Currants and Gooseberries

These two small fruits have experienced a resurgence in popularity in recent years. Both will benefit from mulch's ability to keep soil temperatures down and moisture levels up. Just about any organic mulch will function around currants and gooseberries — straw, leaves, aged manure, sawdust, or whatever. Lay down 2 or 3 inches of these mulches while planting your bushes and replenish annually.

index

Note: Page numbers in *italics* refer to illustrations.

Metric Conversions

Given measurement	To convert it to	Multiply it by
inches	centimeters	2.54
feet	meters	0.305
square feet	square meters	0.092
cubic yards	cubic meters	0.765
pounds	kilograms	0.45
°F	°C	°F − 32 x $\frac{5}{9}$

OTHER STOREY TITLES YOU WILL ENJOY

The Lawn & Garden Owner's Manual, by Lewis and Nancy Hill. This complete guide allows you to diagnose and cure lawn and garden problems, rejuvenate neglected landscaping, and maintain beautiful grounds throughout the year. Advice on hedges, shade trees, lawns, ground covers, perennial beds, vines, and more. 192 pages. Paperback. ISBN 1-58017-214-8.

Let It Rot! The Gardener's Guide to Composting, by Stu Campbell. Gardeners will learn how to recycle waste to create soil-nourishing compost. Contains advice for starting and maintaining a composting system, building bins, and using compost. 160 pages. Paperback. ISBN 1-58017-023-4.

The Vegetable Gardener's Bible, by Edward C. Smith. By integrating four principles — wide rows, organic methods, raised beds, and deep soil — you can cultivate deep, powerful soil that nourishes plants and discourages pests, disease, and weeds. Enjoy gardening as you never have before! 320 pages. Paperback. ISBN 1-58017-212-1.

Secrets to Great Soil, by Elizabeth P. Stell. Create productive soil anywhere with step-by-step instructions for making compost and fertilizers. 224 pages. Paperback. ISBN 1-58017-008-0.

Building a Healthy Lawn: A Safe and Natural Approach, by Stuart Franklin. Includes chapters on mowing, watering, fertilizing, soil building, equipment selection, seeding, weed control, diseases, insects, ground covers, and mulches. 184 pages. Paperback. ISBN 0-88266-518-9.

Squirrel Proofing Your Home & Garden, by Rhonda Massingham Hart. This practical guide is filled with effective tips for keeping squirrels and their relatives from destroying gardens and birdfeeders and invading attics, garages, and basements. 160 pages. Paperback. ISBN 1-58017-191-5.

Carrots Love Tomatoes: Secrets of Companion Planting for Successful Gardening, by Louise Riotte. This complete reference explains which plants nourish the soil, which keep away bugs and pests, and which plants just don't get along. 224 pages. Paperback. ISBN 1-58017-027-7.

Roses Love Garlic, by Louise Riotte. This guide lists hundreds of herbs and flowers with information on how their proximity can maximize the health and yield of vegetable plants, berry bushes, and fruit and nut trees. 256 pages. Paperback. ISBN 1-58017-028-5.

These books and other Storey books are available at your bookstore, farm store, garden center, or directly from Storey Books, Schoolhouse Road, Pownal, Vermont 05261, or by calling 1-800-441-5700. Or visit our Web site at www.storeybooks.com